PEOPLES OF ROMAN BRITAIN

General Editor Keith Branigan
Lecturer in Archaeology in the University of Bristol

CORNOVII

CORITANI

ICENI

TRINOVANTES

SILURES

DOBUNNI

CATUVELLAUNI

ATREBATES

BELGAE

REGNI

CANTIACI

DUROTRIGES

DUMNONII

0   50

miles

THE
REGNI

BARRY CUNLIFFE
Professor of European Archaeology in the University of
Oxford

DUCKWORTH

First published in 1973 by
Gerald Duckworth and Co. Ltd.
43 Gloucester Crescent,
London NW1

Cloth ISBN 0 7156 0669 7
Paper ISBN 0 7156 0699 9

Typeset in Great Britain by
Specialised Offset Services Ltd., Liverpool,
and printed by
Unwin Brothers Ltd.,
Old Woking, Surrey.

Contents

List of Illustrations

Line drawings by Jennifer Gill

1.

Tribal territory and the pre-Roman Iron Age

The territory of the Regni was, and still is, diverse in its physical structure, its economic potential and the distribution of its population. In general terms it can be divided into four zones; three of them, the Weald, the Downs and the coastal strip, are all aligned east to west with the fourth zone, the broad river valleys, cutting at right angles through the other three (fig. 1).

From the point of view of early settlement the Downland strip was the most important — a broad band of chalk six miles wide and over sixty miles long stretching from the edge of the undulating Hampshire chalk uplands to the imposing cliffs of Beachy Head. The whole band dips gently but noticeably to the south. Once it formed part of a great dome which covered the Weald, but the constant action of the rivers eroded away the centre leaving only a fringe of chalk now represented by the North Downs, the Hampshire Downs and the South Downs. The eroded edge stands up as a cliff-like scarp facing into the Weald and forming a formidable barrier to communication. At the western end, the crest reaches almost 900 ft. at Butser Hill near Petersfield; at the east the cliffs of Beachy Head are a little over 500 ft. high. South of the scarp the chalk dips gradually beneath the newer sands and clays of the Hampshire Basin, appearing again only briefly as a minor ruck in the strata to create the hills of Portsdown and Highdown.

The uniformity of the chalk bedrock should not give the impression that the downland offered a single habitat. Weathering and erosion have created a wide variety of

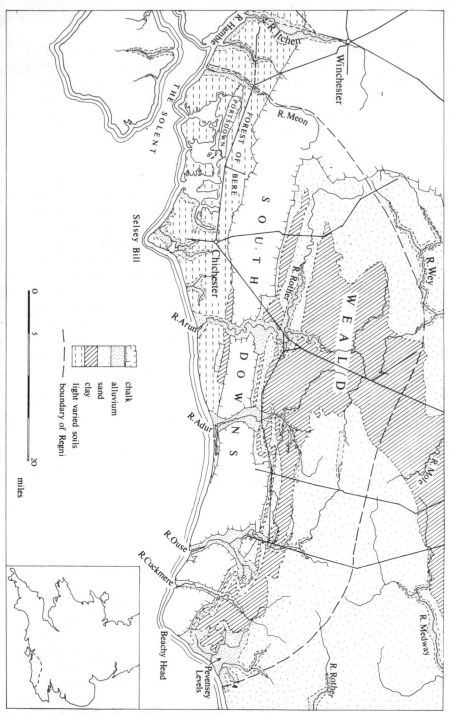

Fig. 1   The territory of the Regni

Winchester

R. Ichen

R. Hamble

R. Meon

PORTSDOWN

FOREST OF BERE

THE SOLENT

Selsey Bill

Chichester

SOUTH

DOWNS

WEALD

R. Rother

R. Wey

R. Mole

R. Arun

R. Adur

R. Medway

R. Ouse

R. Cuckmere

R. Rother

Beachy Head

Pevensey Levels

chalk
alluvium
sand
clay
light varied soils
boundary of Regni

0   5   20
miles

environments. The scarp slope, by virtue of its steepness, is virtually uninhabitable; even now it is given over to rough pasture or wooded hangers. The exposed crests of the ridge must have been too wild and weather-beaten to have supported crops but could have been used intermittently for pasturing livestock when the physical conditions allowed. Further down the dip slope many of the hill crests were overlaid by deposits of clay of varying thickness made up by the residues created by the erosion of the layers above. By the Roman period these clay caps were usually being farmed, but in the preceding periods they were mostly untouched and they would have been left as areas of woodland providing valuable fodder for cattle and pigs.

The Downland strip was dissected by valleys. A few of them, like the Adur, the Arun, the Ouse and the Cuckmere, were wide and difficult to cross, but for the most part the valleys were slight and many would have flowed with streams for only a relatively short season, most of the year remaining dry. The mixture of gravels and silts in the valley floors offered a rich return to those able to cultivate them. So, too, would the thinner soils of the protected valley sides. Within this intricate patchwork of varying landscape features, farming communities once established, spread out, colonizing more and more of the waste until the fields coalesced and the patches of virgin downland gradually shrank.

Along the southern fringe of the Downs the chalk dips beneath the tertiary rocks of the Hampshire Basin — a series of bands of clays and sands which outcrop at their most typical at the extreme western edge of the region north of Portsdown — an area which became known as the Forest of Bere. South of Portsdown and along the coastal plain as far as Brighton these rocks are overlain by varying thicknesses of Quaternary sediments deposited during and immediately following the Glacial period. Over large areas a chalky-gravelly marl, known as coombe rock, forms the basis but is obscured in places by a fine-grained light clay referred to as brickearth. In the final stages many areas of the coastal plain were blanketed by gravel deposits belonging to the successive regressions of the Solent River.

Such a complex geological development has given rise to a

very varied subsoil which in turn has considerably influenced
the settlement pattern. The thick Tertiary clays and the sands
in the west have until recently supported forest and
heathland highly unattractive to the early farmers but no
doubt used by them as pannage for their herds. The spreads
of brickearth and coombe rock, on the other hand, offer a
lighter and more fertile soil which was extensively cultivated
in the Iron Age and Roman period while the gravel terraces
were first settled and farmed on a large scale in the preceding
Bronze Age.

North of the chalk Downs lay the Weald — a vast tract of
clays and sands which remained sparsely occupied until the
sixteenth century, except for the strings of Saxon and
medieval villages which clustered along the rivers. There is
little evidence of settled economy until the builders of a few
hill forts penetrated the area in the Iron Age and men started
to extract iron from the ferruginous sandstones. It would be
wrong to give the impression that the Weald was a totally
desolate area: much of the central part was, but around the
fringes a series of bands of alternating clay and sandstone ran
roughly parallel to the downland scarp up to a bench of
calcarious Upper greensand which lay at the foot of the
scarp slope. This mixture of soils, and in particular the fertile
greensand, was avidly settled in the Roman period and
indeed supported the villa at Bignor — the largest and most
luxurious in the region. The way in which the later Saxon
villages were carefully sited on the greensand bench is an
added indication of its attraction to early settlers.

A number of rivers arose in the Weald, four of them
flowing southwards to the sea in wide valleys, cutting straight
through the chalk Downs and meandering across the coastal
plain. In prehistoric times they would have created serious
hindrance to rapid communication along the Downs but
would have provided some advantage to those seeking a quick
and easy access to the interior by boat. The valley of the
Arun was the widest, being on average three quarters of a
mile across; the others, the Adur, the Ouse and the
Cuckmere, averaged one third of a mile. The wide flood
plains would have been of little use to early corn growers
because of the impossibility of draining them sufficiently for

arable production, but as water meadows they would have provided a valuable addition to the pastoral territory of the neighbouring farmsteads.

Although the coastlands of Hampshire and Sussex are shown on the map (fig. 1) as they are at present, we must remember that the actual configuration of the land has been subject to considerable change. During the last stages of the Glacial period the sea level was much lower and the major rivers flowed in deep valleys relating to that level. As the ice melted the sea gradually rose in relation to the land, causing the wide valleys and estuaries to flood while the upper part of the rivers, regraded to the higher level, flowed more slowly and dropped their load, thus rapidly silting up to create the now familiar wide flood plains of the Sussex rivers.[1] Had there been no other processes at work, a typical coastal landscape would have looked much like the area between Portsmouth and Chichester with a jigsaw puzzle-like relationship between land and sea formed by the gradual drowning of the lowlying coastal plain. Much of the Sussex coast was, however, subjected to erosion by the scouring action of the winds and tides eating into the soft rocks.

The survival of the harbours of the Portsmouth region is due entirely to the protective action of the Isle of Wight, which has so deflected the destructive currents that they do not strike the mainland coast before the region of Selsey Bill. Thereafter the great sweep of the erosive forces is apparent, the sea cutting back as far as the chalk in the region beyond Brighton. The scouring has had another effect — the creation of bars of shingle across the river mouths. This shows particularly clearly at Shoreham at the mouth of the Adur, where the actual outlet of the river to the sea has been deflected for two miles. The formation of partial barriers across the rivers by this process of longshore drift has the added consequence that sediment can more easily accumulate behind, thus speeding up the silting of the river valleys.

The coasts of the western part of the region were not entirely free from the effects of coastal drift in spite of the protection afforded by the Isle of Wight. The tides of the Solent have gradually built up shingle bars across the mouths of the inlets, but the immense volumes of sea water entering and leaving the harbours at each change of tide have ensured the maintenance of deep water channels and have prevented complete blocking.

Sufficient will have been said to show that the creation of the Sussex and Hampshire coast results from a complex of dynamic processes which indeed are still with us. Quite dramatic changes have taken place in the last 2000 years. The Selsey peninsula, which takes the brunt of the erosive forces, has been disappearing at a rapid rate, several feet a year in recent times. At the beginning of the Roman period it must have been far more extensive than it is now. Conversely the great lagoon that once existed on the protected north side of Beachy Head has now totally silted up. In the late Roman period it was navigable up to Pevensey, where the presence of a Roman shore fort implies a nearby anchorage for the fleet. The silting has taken place gradually, the later stages being well attested by medieval documentary records. Portsmouth harbour, protected by the Roman shore fort of Portchester, does not seem to have altered much since the Roman period, except for the erosion of some of the adjacent land. The force of the tides will have been sufficient to have kept it largely silt-free.

Against these localized changes one overall process seems to have begun to take effect during the late Roman period. There is now reasonable evidence to show that the south-east of Britain was subject to a slight overall rise in sea-level. The principal effects of such a change would have been to make the harbours like Pevensey rather more usable, while at the same time causing lowlying coastal areas to flood. An associated result would have been a rise in the water table, forcing the height of the spring line in the Downs to advance — a phenomenon which might well have had some effect on the agricultural potential of land hitherto too far from fresh water to be suitable for regular pastoral activities.

Within this complex and ever-changing landscape the presence of man added another variable.[2] Before about 4000 B.C. the hunter-gatherers who inhabited the area can have had little lasting effect on the landscape except for initiating a gradual process of small-scale deforestation. It used to be thought that these communities lived and hunted only on the sandy soils of the Weald and the Forest of Bere, but it is now clear that their activities spread to the coastal regions and to the Downland as well and must reflect a seasonal and semi-nomadic way of life utilizing the different ecozones as the available food source shifted. Three or four thousand years of seasonal movement by these hunting and gathering communities cannot have failed to have created clearings in the light forest cover but the extent and overall effects of their activities cannot yet be assessed.

The first major changes would have come about as the result of the introduction of farming activities by about 3500 B.C. The exploitation of the Downland by clearing the scrub and introducing the cultivation of barley and wheat, together with the husbanding of cattle and sheep would gradually have led to the opening up of the chalkland, a process which once begun would have been difficult to reverse. Indeed the gradual expansion of this kind of farming, with minor improvements and occasional shifts in the relative significance of the arable and pastoral activities characterized the next four and a half millennia. By the fourth century A.D. mixed farming had spread not only over the entire Downland area but south on to the brickearth soils and north into the fringes of the Weald. The first major reverse came at the beginning of the fifth century A.D., by which time the arable land had begun rapidly to contract.

The exploitation of the food-producing potential led to an increase in population and the first signs of social cohesion, represented in the archaeological record by the appearance of causewayed camps during the latter part of the fourth millennium. There are four in the region under discussion: two, one at the Trundle, near Chichester, and one at Whitehawk, near Brighton, are large, while the other two, Barkhale and Combe Hill, are substantially smaller. It is now generally agreed that causewayed camps served as focal points for Neolithic communities — places where meetings could be held, gifts exchanged and rituals practised. They were in fact the communal centres of tribal society. It is tempting to see in the siting of the two major 'camps', Trundle and Whithawk, the emergence of territories, perhaps with the River Adur serving as a boundary. The development

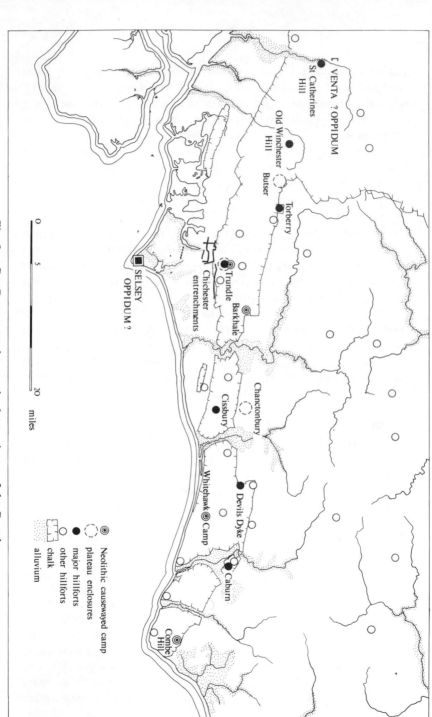

Fig. 2. Pre-Roman settlement in the territory of the Regni

VENTA ?OPPIDUM
St Catherines Hill
Old Winchester Hill
Butser
Torberry
Trundle
Chichester entrenchments
Barkhale
SELSEY OPPIDUM ?
Chanctonbury
Cissbury
Whitehawk Camp
Devils Dyke
Caburn
Combe Hill

⊚ Neolithic causewayed camp
⊚ plateau enclosures
● major hillforts
◌ other hillforts
○
▒ chalk
░ alluvium

0   5   20
miles

of additional centres at Combe Hill and Barkhale might well reflect a growth in population with the consequent fission of the earlier social groupings.

The effects of the so-called Beaker immigrants and folk movements on either side of 2000 B.C. are difficult to assess. There is some possibility that pastoralism became more important while the emphasis of the characteristic Beaker burials of this period is upon the individual, paving the way for the emergence of an aristocratic cast during the first half of the second millennium, which manifests itself in the 'Wessex Culture' burials such as the famous one at Hove with its superb amber cup, stone axe hammer, whetstone and dagger.

How the communal centres fared during this period is unknown, but by the end of the second millennium it would seem that new types of focus had developed. These were essentially large tracts of hill plateaux defined by banks and ditches cutting off the adjacent spurs.[3] This class of monument is relatively little known and considerable doubt still attaches to its date, but the bracket 1500 to 500 is reasonable on the basis of the evidence at present available. One such enclosure would seem to have been constructed around the old causewayed camp on the Trundle.[4] Others are known on Butser Hill,[5] Bow Hill and Chanctonbury Ring (p. 109). While it must be admitted that proof is lacking, it may be suggested that the plateau enclosures provided places of assembly for the tribe at certain times during the year, thus bridging the gap between the Neolithic 'causewayed camps' and the later Iron Age 'hill-forts'.

By the middle of the first millennium many of the more prominent chalk hill tops had become enclosed with ramparts and ditches. Some may have been communal sites, some stock enclosures, others defended habitations. As time went on many of them were abandoned, while a few increased in strength and began to dominate the landscape, until by the beginning of the first century B.C. each block of Downland possessed a major fort (fig. 2). The pattern of development is suggestive of the emergence of a series of strongly centralized tribal groupings, each owing their allegiance to the local fort which presumably contained the agency of goverment, either a single chief or a ruling body.[6]

In the countryside round about, and in particular on the chalk hills, farming communities were by now well established. Indeed, continuity of settlement can in some cases be traced back to before 1000 B.C. The farms varied considerably in size from the village-like clusters of houses at Itford Hill[7] (*c*.1000 B.C.) to the single family units at Chalton[8] (*c*.1300 B.C.). In the later periods, however, the larger type of settlement seems to have become much rarer, possibly because the population was now concentrating on the hill-forts rather than the rural farms.

The principal means of livelihood remained much the same as it had been for 3000 years. Wheat and barley formed the staple crops while cattle, sheep and pigs continued to be husbanded. There were some minor improvements such as the introduction of winter-sown varieties of corn like spelt and hulled barley, and as more fields were carved out of the virgin Downland the flocks of sheep were increased, providing the manure so necessary to maintain fertility. Sheep were preferable to cattle because of their ability to survive for long periods without water — a distinct advantage on the more open parts of the Downs. By about 100 B.C. it might be said that man had finally reached a state of stable equilibrium with his environment.

Much of the best farmland had by now been colonized and settlements were beginning to spread onto the heavier soils of the coastal plain. There are some signs, too, that specialization was developing. Around the fringes of the inlets extensive salt works, some dating back to the third century B.C., were in active production to serve the needs of the growing population, while in the Weald there sprang up settlements of specialists engaged in the extraction of iron from the ferruginous sandstone. Iron was by now in common use for tools and weapons alike.

The geography of the civitas

It is now necessary to look in more detail at the problems posed by considering the limits of tribal territories. It has already been suggested that the large hill-forts represented the focal points of chiefdoms, each fort occupying the centre of a distinct geographical region, usually bounded by rivers (fig. 2). If this is so, there were about seven individual units east of the River Meon. The political relationships between the territories cannot be known, but in all probability they would have been in some kind of treaty relationship with each other (or alternatively, of course, in conflict). A study of the pottery goes some way towards suggesting the extent of these larger groupings.

The ceramics of the second century to early first century B.C. fall into two distinct groups which can be defined on stylistic grounds, largely on the basis of their decoration.[9] Broadly speaking, the pottery found to the east of the Arun relies more on curvelinear decoration incorporating patterns composed of arcs and interlocking swags, while the vessels found over a wide territory from the Arun to the Test are more restrained, making use of simple linear designs often combining zones of close-spaced diagonal lines with horizontal rows of dots. Although detailed petrographic analysis has not yet been undertaken, it may well be that each style will be found to have originated in a single production centre, as was the case elsewhere in Britain at this time. Taken on its simplest level, the distribution area of a well-defined style of pottery should represent a region within which certain levels of contact were maintained and might therefore be thought to reflect a degree of political unity. If this is so, the region divides into two somewhere about the line of the River Arun. As we will see, the division holds good in the later period as well.

Throughout the period from *c.*120-60 B.C. the south-east of Britain received a body of immigrants from the adjacent continental lowlands. Caesar refers briefly to the situation in a now famous passage in which he describes the Belgae who, he says, came to raid and stayed to sow. Recent detailed work on the coinage of this period has shown that the south-east received a series of intrusions of continental coinage which may represent the near continuous arrival of 'Belgic' immigrants over a period of sixty years or so — a movement resulting first from dislocations caused by the warlike activities of the Cimbri and the Teutones, who forced their way through Gaul at the end of the second century, and later by the disturbing activities of Caesar himself during his campaigns south of the Rhine. The exact interpretation to be placed on the coin evidence is debatable. Some would see each new type of Gallo-Belgic coinage as representing a new wave of immigrants, but it could equally well be argued that the appearance of a coin type merely reflected a political or economic factor and need not imply folk movement.[10] At any event, it can safely be said that contact with the continent increased dramatically in the half century or so before Caesar's invasions.

The earliest coins arrived in Britain before 100 B.C. One group, the Gallo-Belgic A from the Somme area, are found in Kent and Essex, while the approximately contemporary Gallo-Belgic B issues from the Somme-Lower Seine region cluster in the Thames region. It is tempting to equate the appearance of these types with Caesar's Belgic invaders fleeing from the rampagings of the Cimbri and Teutones and setting up political domination over the indigenous communities. A number of these Gallo-Belgic issues have also been found in Sussex, but their occurrence here need imply little more than trade with other areas of Britain.

The next continental type to appear, Gallo-Belgic C, is more puzzling. Only a few examples are found, generally scattered over the south-east, but the type lies at the beginning of a series of local British developments. One possibility is that these coins, dating to *c*. 95-65 B.C., are a reflection of the political power of the great Belgic chieftain Diviciacus, who was remembered by Caesar's envoys as overlord of Gaul and Britain. An explanation in these terms would account for the evident prestige implied by the numerous localized British coinages which the Gaulish type inspired.[11] Within the area here discussed there was one British development called British A. The known coins cluster upon the west Sussex coastal plain, with a few examples extending into the western chalkland areas of Hampshire. While too much weight cannot be given to such slight evidence, it may be significant that these coins occupy much the same territory as one of the groups of decorated pottery mentioned above (p. 11), and as we will see (below,

p. 14) the territory maintained its identity during the later ceramic development of the region.

So far the intrusive coinages had had little effect on the Sussex area, but between *c.*80 and 50 B.C. a new coin type, a geometric quarter stater known as Gallo-Belgic D, appeared in Britain with a strong coastal distribution spreading from Kent to Hampshire and giving rise in Sussex to a local development called British O. The meaning of this concentration is uncertain but it is evident that close contacts were now emerging between the southern coastal areas of Britain and the continental mainland.

Some time in the 60s or 50s a new wave of coinage, Gallo-Belgic E, flooded into south-eastern Britain, concentrating in Essex, the Thames valley and Sussex. So extensive is the distribution that it points to intrusive elements rather than just trade. This may indeed be the archaeological manifestation of Caesar's remark that the chiefs of the Bellovaci took refuge in Britain from his advance into their territory in 57 B.C. It seems that in Kent and Essex the aristocratic influx was accompanied by a widespread folk movement, introducing specialized cremation rites and a new style of fine wheel-turned pottery. In Sussex on the other hand there is very little evidence for cultural changes of any kind, apart from the acceptance of the new coinage. Interpretation is, once more, difficult: folk movement into Sussex is unproven, but some kind of political domination may well have been established over the region by the leaders of the communities settled in Kent and the Thames area.

In 55 and in 54 B.C. Julius Caesar led substantial military expeditions to Britain, but it was against the leaders of the kingdoms in Kent, Essex and Hertfordshire that his energies were pitted: the region south of the Weald remained untouched. During the preparations for his invasions Caesar made use of an Atrebatic king called Commius, who seems to have been known and generally respected by the British leaders. Commius returned to the continent with the army in 54 B.C. and remained in allegiance with the Roman authorities, who were now consolidating their hold over newly-conquered Gaul, but in 52 B.C. he suddenly changed sides and joined the great Gaulish king Vercingetorix in his

devastating rebellion against Rome. As the rebellion began to
fail Commius was forced to flee, only narrowly escaping with
his life when, by a trick, he managed to elude the Roman army
and sail to Britain.

The development of the coinage appears to represent
something of this event, for at about this time a new type,
Gallo-Belgic F, is found in small quantities in the south. The
actual numbers are unimpressive but the type gives rise to a
local development called British Q, the distribution of which
concentrates on Sussex and the middle Thames area. These
British Q coins, depicting on their reverse sides the characteristic triple-tailed horse, are the prototypes from which the
first inscribed coins of Commius develop. The sequence,
then, suggests first that the Gallo-Belgic F coins were
introduced soon after 50 B.C. by Commius and his followers,
and second that the Commius who fled from Caesar's troops
is the Commius who turns up in Britain. While both
conclusions seem reasonable it should always be remembered
that they are only assumptions and cannot be regarded as
proven.

If the inscribed coins of Commius are taken to approxi-
mate to the extent of the kingdom over which he ruled, his
territory must have spread from Beachy Head to the
Salisbury Avon and from the Berkshire Downs to the
Channel coast. This was the territory of the Atrebates at its
most extensive. Within this sweep it is possible to distinguish
three constituent groups on the basis of pottery typology.[12]
Over the western area, roughly covering the Wiltshire Downs,
pottery was well made on a wheel, the forms deriving some
influences from ceramics of the 'Belgic' areas to the north. In
the centre, extending as far east as the Arun, the vessels
though wheel-turned were simpler and owed far more to
localized native traditions. East of the Arun even more
native-looking pottery survived in the form of globular jars
with elaborate arc-and-swag curvilinear designs. The survival
of the strong indigenous undercurrent in this last group is
surprising in view of its close proximity to the more elaborate
pottery of Kent: the implications must be that it reflects a
degree of isolation. Too much significance should not be
attached to the variations between these three ceramic zones,

since at best they represent spheres of localized contact and marketing. What do stand out are the sharp differences between the Atrebatic styles and the pottery of the surrounding tribes of the Durotriges, the Catuvellauni and the Cantiaci. It would seem, therefore, that the distribution of Atrebatic coinage was directly reflected by the marketing patterns of a distinctive ceramic tradition. In other words, politico-economic boundaries can probably be recognized in the archaeological record.

With the advent of inscribed coinage and the proximity of the literate Roman world, the broad outlines of Atrebatic politics can be reconstructed.[13] Commius ruled for about thirty years until *c*.20 B.C., when he was succeeded by Tincommius, apparently his son. Tincommius ruled much the same territory as his father and seems to have maintained his inherited anti-Roman position until some time soon after 16 B.C., when he suddenly abandoned the old style of coin design and introduced a Romanized version based on a type issued by the emperor Augustus between 15 and 12 B.C. The new issues are so close in design to the Roman originals that the dies from which they were struck may well have been the work of a Roman engraver. This change would seem to reflect the growth of a pro-Roman feeling among the Atrebates, which may have developed as the result of treaty negotiations between the two states. That some of the British kingdoms had indeed established friendly relations with Rome is implied by a poem of Horace published by 13 B.C., in which he refers to suppliant Britons visiting the court of Augustus.

Some time just before 7 B.C. Tincommius made good use of his relationship with Rome by fleeing from Britain to the protection of the emperor. Why he felt it expedient to depart must remain unknown, but inter-tribal rivalry provides a possible context. He was immediately succeeded by Eppillus, another of the sons of Commius. For a few years Eppillus continued to issue coins from a mint at Silchester (*Calleva*), styling himself REX in good Roman lettering as if to emphasise Roman recognition of his kingly status, but on the evidence of his coinage he was eventually ousted from his kingdom, to reappear in Kent about A.D. 1. The reason for his exodus may well have been the same dynastic squabbling which caused the departure of his brother Tincommius a few years earlier. Eppillus was in his turn replaced by Verica, who also claimed to be a son of Commius and who was to rule the Atrebates for just over forty years until the Roman conquest.

It was during Verica's long reign that substantial areas of the old Atrebatic territory were lost. The northern capital at Calleva was first to go, presumably as the result of the aggressive activities of the powerful Catuvellauni who were rapidly developing expansionist tendencies. By about A.D. 20 a Catuvellaunian ruler, Epaticus, was minting coins from the old capital and thereafter Catuvellaunian coins dominate the area as far south as the River Kennet. How far the original kingdom was eroded away by direct conquest or by fragmentation is difficult to say, but the bulk of Verica's coins are found in Sussex and south-east Hampshire, extending west to the line of the Test or Salisbury Avon. The north had been totally lost.

By the beginning of the first century A.D. most of the hill-forts within the Atrebatic area had long been abandoned. The farmsteads, on the other hand, continued to flourish and expand, particularly into areas of heavier soil, some of them achieving considerable size and complexity — sufficient to justify the title of village. This process of decentralization can only mean that the old order was being superseded. In social terms it is clear that the chiefdoms, represented by the forts, had been replaced by a different style of government, which may have resulted from the upheavals consequent upon the folk movements early in the first century B.C. Added to this, there must have been other widespread changes in south-eastern Britain brought about as contacts with the Roman world developed, following Caesar's conquest of Gaul.

With petty chiefdoms giving way to states ruled by kings, the need for scattered hill-forts disappeared and there developed in their stead large urban centres or *oppida*, which would have served as the site of the tribal mint and possibly the king's court. Towards the end of the first century B.C. the Atrebates possessed three such centres: Silchester (*Calleva*,[14] Winchester (*Venta*), and one located somewhere in the Chichester-Selsey region. Silchester soon passed into the hands of the Catuvellauni and the fate of Winchester is difficult to determine, but the Chichester-Selsey oppidum seems to have remained the focus of Atrebatic power until the last.

The exact location of the inhabited area is inknown, but it is generally thought to have been sited south of the present Selsey Bill, on land subsequently eroded away by the sea leaving only a scatter of gold coins to be found on the beach. This may well be so, but an alternative possibility is that it might lie somewhere close to, or even beneath, the later Roman town of Chichester. A third alternative, that the centre was established first at Selsey and later moved to Chichester, cannot be ruled out. Some light may be thrown on the subject after the publication of the great mass of material recovered by excavation from the earliest levels of the town. Until then the question must remain open.

Wherever the focus of the *oppidum* will prove to be, it is clear that it was defended in the same style as the Catuvellaunian capital at Camulodunum, with a series of massive banks and ditches running for miles across the countryside.[15] The intention seems to have been to strengthen the landward approaches to the Selsey peninsula and Chichester harbour, using earthworks where the land was open and relying on the densely wooded river valleys to guard the flanks. The main earthworks ran from the stream flowing into Bosham harbour, across the gravel coastal plain to the River Lavant, which at this time joined with Pagham Rife and entered the sea at Pagham harbour. An additional earthwork extended the line eastwards for some miles to the valley of Aldingbourne Rife, another south-flowing stream. As the plan (fig. 3) will show, the original area of land thus protected was considerable, but later modifications tended to focus defensive strength on the Fishbourne-Chichester region as if to suggest that the urban nucleus lay somewhere here by the closing decades of the pre-Roman period.

The wealth of the late Atrebatic kingdom can be gauged by the number of coin hoards found within the territory.[16] Altogether some seven hoards amounting to more than 335 coins are recorded, of which the largest single collection is from the shore between Wittering and Selsey. Here some 265 coins have been picked up, the numbers suggesting to some writers that they are part of one or more scattered hoards. An alternative view is that they represent the debris of a mint belonging to the supposed *oppidum* — an interpretation which gains some support from the discovery of fragments of waste gold in the same area. The Selsey collection, whatever its true origin, was composed largely of Sussex types and coins of the Atrebatic dynasty. This contrasts noticably with a hoard found at Portsmouth in 1830, which contained coins of the Durotriges, the Iceni and an Armorican tribe called the Baiocasses. The Portsmouth hoard looks far more like the collection of a merchant than the savings of a local aristocrat. The other Sussex hoards, from Bognor, Ashdown Forest, Birling, Alfriston and Lancing Down, were all local in content and, as far as the records go, the numbers of coins in each hoard were small. One notable fact is that three of them contained late issues of Verica, suggesting deposition towards the middle of the first century A.D., perhaps in the troubled times in A.D. 42 and 43 when the departure of Verica and the arrival of the Roman army must have caused some feelings of unrest.

Matters came to a head in A.D. 40 when rumours reached Britain of a threatened Roman invasion led by the emperor Gaius. The situation must have occasioned considerable internal conflict in the country, not only between the pro- and anti- Roman tribes but also within the ranks of those who were in treaty relations with Rome. To make matters worse, Cunobelin, the old king of the Catuvellauni, died and was replaced by his two sons Togodumnus and Caratacus, both of whom initiated a new expansionist policy. During the unrest which followed, Verica fled to Rome, no doubt to solicit the emperor's support for his cause. Whether his flight was the result of external aggression or internal dissent we will never know.

The archaeology of the crucial years, between the threat of attack by Gaius and its actuality under Claudius three years later, offers some vague impression of the final political line-up.[17] Between the rivers Meon and Ouse there is no trace at all to suggest that the old hill-forts were brought back into defensive order after their abandonment in the first century B.C., but west of the Meon and east of the Ouse there are indisputable signs of re-defence. At the Caburn in the east the ditch was redug and the rampart heightened. The same happened at Danebury in the west, while at the nearby site of Boscombe Down West a new double-ditched defensive enclosure was constructed, and close by at Bury Hill near Andover the old hill-fort was updated with multivalate defences. The inescapable conclusion must be that, west of the Meon or Itchen, Verica's territories re-aligned themselves with their anti-Roman neighbours, the Dobunni and the Durotriges, while the small block of Downland east of the Ouse joined the anti-Roman tribes of Kent. Thus all that was left of the kingdom, still maintaining its pro-Roman attitude, was a much shrunken area centred on the capital. Surrounded by enemies and with the old king gone, the future must have looked decidedly uncertain.

2.

History: A.D. 43-367

In the late spring of A.D. 43 the Roman army embarked at Boulogne to begin their long-awaited conquest of Britain. They sailed at night, Dio says, in three detachments so as not to be held up unnecessarily on landing.[1] Exactly how to interpret this statement is uncertain, but since it is highly unlikely that the commander, Aulus Plautius, would have allowed his force to be fragmented for too long at this crucial juncture, it is more reasonable to suppose that the three-pronged attack was merely an expedient to facilitate landing and that the force soon concentrated before marching inland towards their first great battle on the Medway. The precise locations of two of the three bridgeheads are so far undefined, but one, perhaps the main one, was at Richborough. The others must have been nearby, for widely spaced landings would have held no advantage if the intention behind the three-pronged attack was simply to speed up disembarkation.

The first battle of the Medway was a resounding Roman success. Togodumnus was killed and Caratacus forced to flee. The army was then free to push on to the Thames, cross it and, led for the occasion by the emperor himself, to rampage through Catuvellaunian territory, finally destroying its capital at Camulodunum. Within little more than a month of landing, the south-east was firmly in Roman hands.

How the old Atrebatic enclave fared throughout this period remains unknown. The territory, however, occupied a crucial position in serving as a buffer between the hostile tribes of the south-west (the Durotriges and Dobunni) and the initial theatre of Roman campaigning in Kent. Its significance can hardly have passed unnoticed by the Roman generals planning the attack. The obvious response to the situation would have been to send a small detachment into the area at the earliest opportunity to support the pro-Roman faction and thus to ensure that the situation remained stable while the army gained control of Kent. We will never know if this was done or, if so, precisely when — it simply remains a strong probability.

It must have been at this stage, if not before, that Tiberius Claudius Cogidubnus made his appearance. He is known only from a brief reference in Tacitus' *Agricola* and an inscription from Chichester, but there can be little doubt that he was a man of considerable significance who was to dominate the local scene for at least thirty years.[2] That he was a client king is established, but when and how he came to office is not. He was, however, probably confirmed in power at the very beginning of the invasion and he may even have been given military support: that he was allowed to remain is a sign of his effectiveness.

The origins of Cogidubnus are obscure. His name belies his native pedigree, but since he appears never to have minted coins he is unlikely to have been a king before the invasion. The simplest explanation is that he was a member of the ruling household who was elevated to kingship by the Roman authorities. While they could have brought the ageing Verica back, always supposing that he was still alive, it would have been preferable to implant a younger man. Indeed, if Verica had been forced to flee by local malcontents, a change of leadership would have been desirable. One further speculation which holds some attraction is that Cogidubnus might have been a member of the Atrebatic ruling caste raised from childhood in Rome, a descendant perhaps of Epillus or Tincommius, both of whom had fled to the safety of the emperor's court. The policy of rearing aristocratic young barbarians in the Roman tradition was well established and had evident political advantages when seen against the imperial aspirations of the early empire. Some such explanation could also account for the remarkable success which Cogidubnus showed in Romanizing his kingdom so rapidly. But these speculations, while attractive, remain unproved.

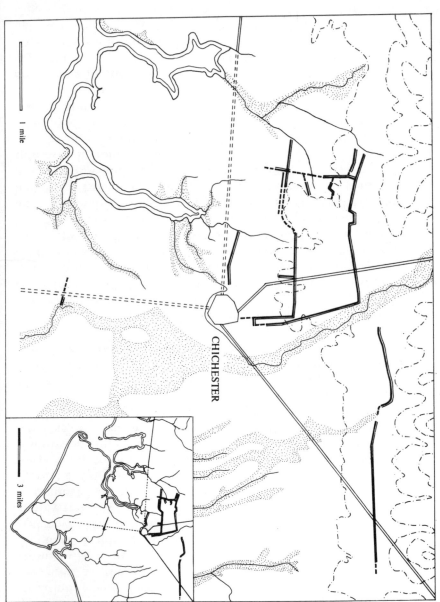

1 mile

3 miles

CHICHESTER

Fig. 2   The *oppidum* at Chichester

According to Tacitus certain estates were returned to king Cogidubnus, who, he says, 'remained faithful down to the time I can remember'.[3] This single sentence raises the whole problem of the boundaries of the kingdom and indeed of its name under Roman government. We can begin by eliminating the area beyond the Meon, for at an early date the Romans had established a cantonal capital at Winchester (*Venta*) which served as the market town of the *civitas Belgarum*. Allowing *Venta* to have an adequate economic hinterland, it must be supposed that the territory between the Itchen and Meon belonged to the town. The concept of a *civitas Belgarum* was artificially imposed upon the old tribal structure by the Roman administration, quite possibly in an attempt to isolate those parts of the Atrebates and Dobunni who had shown opposition at the time of the invasion.

At the opposite end of the region was the area beyond the Ouse which appears to have taken an anti-Roman line in A.D. 43 (p. 18). It would have made good sense geographically to include it in the kingdom. This might, in fact, have been one of the estates which Tacitus says was returned to Cogidubnus. The northern boundary is impossible to define with any accuracy, but the centre of the Weald makes a natural geographical divide: accordingly the limit taken here is the watershed between the rivers flowing north to the Thames and those flowing south to the Channel. This has the advantage of skirting the natural economic hinterlands of Silchester (*Calleva*), London, Rochester (*Durobrivae*) and Canterbury (*Durovernum*) (fig. 13). It also omits a substantial area of the eastern Weald, assuming it to belong to the civitas of the *Cantiaci*, an assumption based on the road system which clearly links this area to the principal urban centres of the *Cantiaci*. The only limit which might be thought to be in serious doubt is that which excludes the area from the North Downs to the Thames. In terms of marketing, this region is clearly dependent upon London and however it was administered it can hardly be regarded as an integral part of the kingdom. One final omission must be justified — the Isle of Wight. The reasons for this are twofold: first its inhabitants were hostile to the Roman advance, since Vespasian had to take the island presumably by force,[4] and secondly its natural communications are with the land of the *civitas Belgarum.*

Under Roman domination the original territory of the Atrebates was split into three cantons: the Atrebates, centred on Silchester; the Belgae, centred on Winchester; and the kingdom of Cogidubnus. The name of the king's tribe has been a matter of debate for some time.[5] Ptolemy calls the people *Regni*, while the name of the principal town, Chichester, is given as *Regno* in the Antonine Itinerary and as *Navimago Regentium* in the Ravenna Cosmography. Broadly speaking there are two interpretations: one suggests that the name derives from the Latin word *Regnum* (kingdom) and the tribe are therefore *Regnenses* (the people of the kingdom), the other suggestion is that *Regni* is a Celtic word, like the Gaulish *Regin* or the Old Welsh *Regin*, originating from a British word *Regini* meaning 'the proud ones, the stiff ones'. This last explanation is the more acceptable since the first is based on assumptions and unsupported emendations which now seem doubtful.

The negotiations which led to the establishment of the Regni under their king Cogidubnus must have taken place at the very beginning of the invasion period, but the kingdom still had an important part to play in the conquest. As soon as Camulodunum had been taken and the military presence established, the army fanned out across the country towards the Jurassic ridge which was soon developed as a frontier zone stretching from Exeter to Lincoln. The Second Legion, under its young commander Vespasian, was given the task of subduing the south-west. Suetonius records that he took the Isle of Wight, overcame two powerful tribes and destroyed more than twenty fortified native settlements.[6] The tribes concerned were the Durotriges and very probably the communities living in Wiltshire and Somerset, who were soon lumped together under the title of Belgae. There is ample archaeological evidence of the campaign, including the dramatic results of the attacks on the hill-forts of Hod Hill and Maiden Castle, as well as the establishment of Roman forts at strategic points like Hod Hill and Waddon Hill.

To mount the south-western campaign, Vespasian probably made use of the client kingdom, to provide not only a safe retreat, if necessary, but also a good harbour on which to

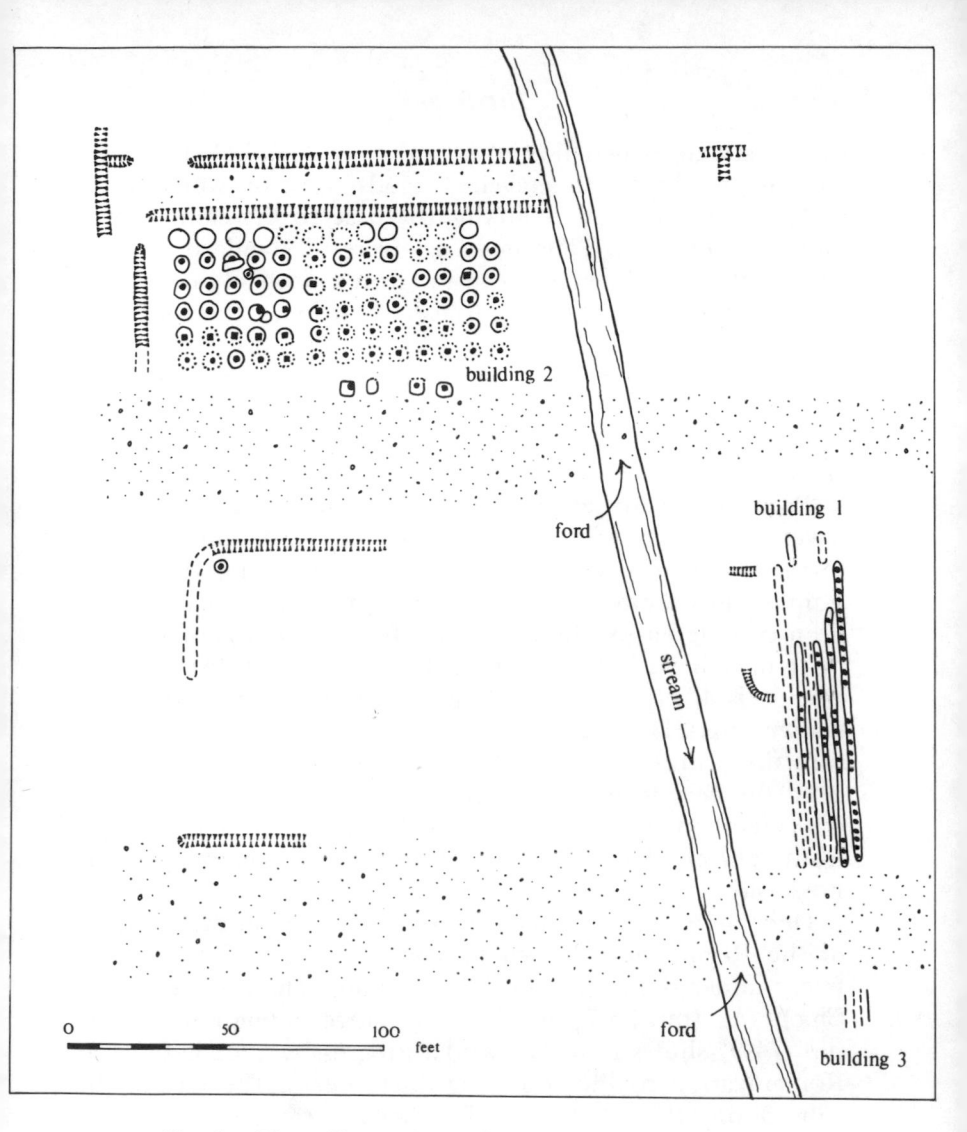

Fig. 4.　The military phase of occupation at Fishbourne

base the sea-borne support for the thrust. The location chosen for the camp was probably Chichester, with the supply base sited nearby at Fishbourne at the head of a wide and well-protected inlet. The military remains from Chichester are described below (p. 49) and need not be considered here. At Fishbourne three store houses have been discovered (fig. 4), all built of timber and placed on either side of the stream which flowed into the creek-end.[7] They were well served by wide gravelled roads, one of which leads eastwards — presumably linking the base to the camp a mile away at Chichester. The buildings were of standard military construction designed to keep the stores, probably corn, well clear of the damp ground-surface. A little to the south lay harbour works, the details of which are still obscure. Military artifacts were not plentiful at Fishbourne, but included various buckles and belt plates and an iron ballista head. To these must be added a legionary's helmet dredged out of the creek in the last century (fig. 5).

From the Chichester-Fishbourne base Vespasian would have been able to mount an effective attack, sending the bulk of the troops to advance by land, while supporting them with supplies and reinforcements by sea. The campaign may have been completed by the end of the fighting season of A.D. 43 or it may have been renewed in the spring of 44; in either case it is likely that the camp at Chichester served as the winter quarters for the legion. How long the troops were to stay there presents a problem. They may have departed for good the next year, but the possibility remains that the camp was maintained at least until A.D. 47, by which time the frontier zone had been established along the line of the Fosseway.

Once a frontier had been created well beyond the territory of the Regni, the tribe would have been allowed to develop freely under the leadership of their king. The evidence from Chichester (pp. 53-7) and from the surrounding countryside (pp. 74-9) shows that spectacular progress was made towards Romanization in the following thirty years. The fate of the tribe during the rebellion of Boudicca is unrecorded but it is probable that Cogidubnus was able to keep his people steadfast throughout the uprising, providing a welcome oasis of calm when much of the rest of the province was in uproar.

At some stage during his reign Cogidubnus was given the remarkable title of *legatus augusti*, recorded on an inscription found at North Street in Chichester (fig. 6)[8]. To elevate a client king to the rank of imperial legate was rare indeed, and would only be done in the most exceptional circumstances. One explanation is that Cogidubnus received this honour in

Fig. 5. A legionary helmet found in Chichester harbour

69 or 70 for his support of Vespasian in the scramble for the throne following the death of Nero in A.D. 68. The two men would almost certainly have known each other from the days of the invasion, twenty-five years previously, and it is quite possible that in 69 when the leadership was in balance Cogidubnus gave his personal support to Vespasian's cause, bringing a large body of influential public opinion in Britain with him. If so, his judgment was shrewd, for when Vespasian emerged triumphant the supporters of the new emperor would have been well rewarded.

As an imperial legate, the king would have carried out a wide range of administrative duties. With the new military initiative in the north requiring the constant attention of the Governor, it is possible that certain affairs of state may have devolved upon him. At any event, the vast new palace erected at Fishbourne in the mid-70s (pp. 80-2) would have been a most suitable residence for a man of this exalted rank. The centrally-placed audience chamber with its vaulted roof and domed semi-circular throne recess is a visual reminder of both the status and the duties of its owner. It is an attractive speculation to see the vast palace as the final home of this venerable old man, the last survivor in power of the old

Fig. 6.   The Cogidubnus Inscription from Chichester

native aristocracy and at the same time a trusted servant, and perhaps friend, of the Emperor.

Cogidubnus probably lived long enough to see the neighbouring town of Chichester undergo a phase of large-scale replanning, including the erection of its principal monumental buildings; he may also have been responsible for the construction of the road stations at Hardham, Alfoldean and Iping to ensure the safe and efficient conveyance of the imperial post, but he is unlikely to have outlived the last decade of the first century, for even if he was as young as his early 30s at the time of the invasion he would have been approaching 80 years old by A.D. 90. On his death, the kingdom would have been absorbed into the administrative framework of the province and the Regni would have ceased thenceforth to be a privileged people.

Much of the second century was uneventful, but the troubles in the north and the west in the decade on either side of A.D. 200 may have encouraged the southern towns to defend themselves with earthworks and later stone walls (pp. 57-60). Alternatively enclosure may have been simply a result of civic pride after Caracalla had granted citizenship to all free-born provincials. At any event, Chichester followed the tradition of its neighbours.

Little is known of British provincial history throughout the third century but there is no reason to suppose that any major reverses of fortune were experienced by the Regni until the 270s, by which time the coastal regions of the south-east were beginning to feel the effects of barbarian raids. One sign of the growing insecurity is the great increase in the number of coin hoards hidden at this time. Statistics show that between 253 and 268 there were on average 1.6 hoards deposited per year; between 268 and 270, 11.5 per year; between 270 and 275, 25.6 per year; and between 275 and 282, 5.9 per year. On this showing the peak of the panic was the early 270s. It is, perhaps, significant that this coincided with the great influx of Barbarians into Gaul in 276 when fifty or sixty of the Gaulish towns fell to the raiders. The situation was restored by Probus in the following year, as a result of which detachments of captured Burgundians and Vandals were sent to Britain to serve with the army. But even with law and order re-established in Gaul, Britain was not safe. By the mid 280s the seas had become infested with pirates to such an extent that the central government appointed a Belgian sailor, Carausius, 'to rid the seas of Belgica and Armorica of pirates'.[9] His orders are significant, for they show that the pirates who had already made themselves a nuisance in the North Sea ('the seas of Belgica') had now broken through the straits of Dover and were causing havoc in the English Channel ('the seas of Armorica').

The Barbarian attack on Gaul and the pirates nearer at home cannot have failed to strike fear into the hearts of the Regni, particularly those living near the coast. A large number of coin hoards have been found in the area, buried during the period 275-87 or thereabouts.[10] Of the three hoards from Eastbourne one ends with issues of Aurelian (*c.*275), the other two with Probus (*c.*282). At Newhaven two hoards extend to issues of Tetricus (*c.*273) and Probus (*c.*282) respectively. The great Selsey hoard contains coins up to Victorinus (*c.*271) and, nearby at Almodington, coins of Gallienus (*c.*268) end the series. The Watersfield hoard near Pulborough was buried sometime after the coins of Quintillus (*c.*270) came into use; the 1000 coins from the Rottingdean hoard end with Tetricus II (*c.*275) while the hoard from Linchmere was not buried until *c.*289-90. Finally, there are three remarkably similar hoards from Goring, Hove and Worthing, which seem to have been hidden late in the reign of Probus (276-82). These thirteen hoards are a dramatic reminder of panic which must have pervaded the area, particularly among the communities living in the unprotected coastal regions.

Whether or not actual raids took place is less certain, but the Roman buildings at Fishbourne, near Chichester, and Preston Park, now in the suburbs of Brighton, were both destroyed by fire in the late third century and were not re-occupied. The fires could, of course, have been accidental, but their occurrence at this time is at least suggestive of more violent causes. That actual raids were taking place is implied by the accusation, made by the enemies of Carausius, that he allowed the pirates to land and collect booty and then met them at sea to share the loot. Even if the story were vicious propaganda, it would only have been credible if raiding and looting were a reality.

The appointment of Carausius to the command of the fleet in 285 followed his successful campaigns against the Bagaudae of Gaul, a confederation of deserters and disenchanted peasants who were roaming the countryside.[11] Later in the same year, however, he broke with the central government and set up an empire of his own based on Britain. He was to hold the province until his assassination at the hands of Allectus, one of his commanders, in 293. During these seven years of independence the emperor of the west, Maximian, was powerless. He had managed to amass a navy in 288 to fight against Carausius, but in the following year he suffered defeat at sea and thereafter abandoned any attempt at re-conquest. Carausius responded by making overtures of friendship which are recorded on the legends of coins – a common propaganda medium in the late Roman period.

Carausius was clearly in a position of strength. Holding Britain and the adjacent French coast and with a powerful navy strengthened with a considerable Barbarian element patrolling the Channel, he was firmly in control. He had inherited a system of coastal defences spreading from the Wash to Kent, which no doubt he modified and brought up to date. Several of the forts, Richborough, Dover, Lympne and Portchester, were built in the last quarter of the third century, either by Carausius himself or a few years earlier, perhaps under the authority of Probus: all were now occupied on a large scale, serving as bases for marines and frontier troops alike.[12]

Portchester (fig. 7),[13] was constructed on a virgin site, on a low promontory of brickearth projecting into the upper reaches of Portsmouth harbour, a large and easily protected expanse of water eminently suitable for the amassing of a substantial fleet. The fort consisted of an almost square enclosure of about 9 acres in extent, protected by a massively-built flint and mortar wall some 10 ft. thick and in excess of 20 ft high. The two main gates were situated in the centres of the east and west walls, with subsidiary posterns in equivalent positions in the north and south walls. The

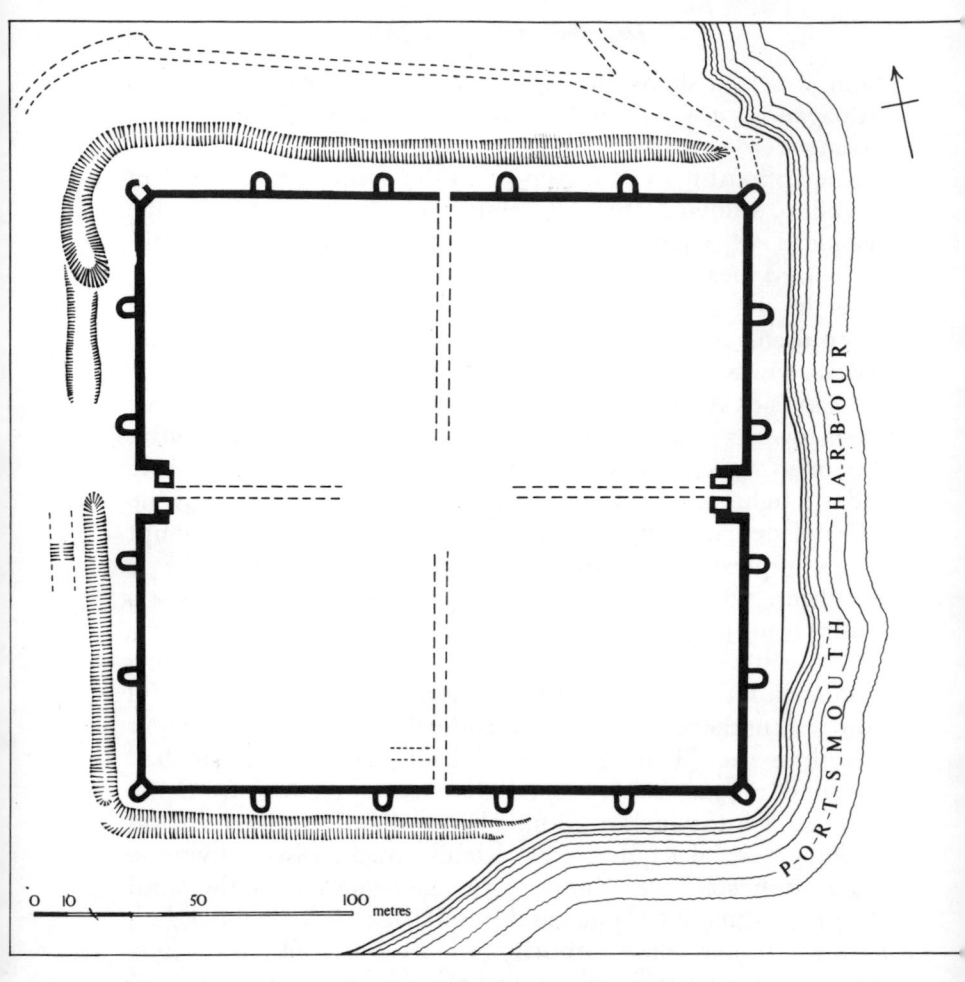

Fig. 7.   Plan of the shore fort at Portchester

exterior wall-faces were provided with projecting D-shaped bastions regularly spaced, four along each wall with diagonal bastions on each of the corners. In front was a double ditch-system.

The emphasis of the architecture was on defence. The bastions, for example, were floored across with timber to serve as fighting platforms and probably supported artillery of some kind, while the double ditches would have kept any would-be attackers within easy killing range. The main gates were very carefully designed to be virtually impregnable. The full 10 ft. width of the fort wall was inturned to form a courtyard, at the head of which the gate, flanked by two guard-chambers, was constructed; above, one must suppose the existence of a tower with fighting platform. The strength of the defences is a dramatic illustration of the new problems which the empire was facing.

Whether or not the late third-century forts were constructed by Probus or Carausius, there can be no doubt that Carausius would have used them as an essential part of his defences against threat of attack by the central government. They would thus have served the joint function of housing the troops to be used against pirates and providing strong reserves of troop concentrations in the event of an Imperial expedition. The question which immediately arises is: is Portchester the only fort in the territory of the Regni? The distance between it and its nearest contemporary neighbour, Lympne, is more than 100 miles, far too great to allow for the effective cover of the intervening coast. Either one supposes that there are forts between still to be identified, or the system entailed only the use of isolated strong-points from which patrols could issue forth. Since a combination of coastal erosion and silting may well have obscured or destroyed any fort along the length of the Sussex coastal plain between Selsey and Beachy Head, the question must remain open.

The interior arrangements of the fort at Portchester are becoming clearer as the result of current excavations. Gravelled streets with central gutters ran from all four gates and each quarter thus defined was further divided (fig. 9). The buildings, where they survived, appeared to be of sill-beam construction with floors of timber and occasionally mortar. One surprising discovery was that during the late third-century phase of occupation considerable quantities of rubbish were tipped in heaps against the inner faces of the fort walls: such a practice would hardly have been tolerated under the old military order and must imply far-reaching changes in organization. So far, however, the ground plan has little information to offer concerning the status or even the arrangement of the individual units of the garrison.

In 293 Constantius was appointed by Diocletian as one of

Fig. 8.   An aerial view of Portchester Castle

Fig. 9.   A surfaced Roman road inside Portchester

the two Caesars to succeed to the throne on his retirement. Constantius immediately set about the problems of the break-away state. He first captured Carausius' main base at Boulogne and then began to construct a fleet. The loss of the continental foot-hold was a blow to Carausius' prestige: within a few months he was murdered by his finance minister, Allectus, who was to maintain British independence for a further three years.

In 296 Constantius launched his attack for which Allectus must have been prepared. One arm of the invasion force, led by Asclepiodotus, outflanked the British fleet somewhere near the Isle of Wight and landed on the coast, presumably in the region of Southampton Water, whence it marched inland towards London. Allectus' army, impressed by the presence of the second arm of Constantius' fleet which appeared in the Straits of Dover, had concentrated in Kent. When news of the southern landing reached them, Allectus marched west to meet the invading army somewhere in north Hampshire, only to be soundly defeated and killed. The remnants of his force, composed of regular troops together with a number of Frankish mercenaries, fell back towards London but were prevented from looting the capital by the arrival of Constantius' forces. Britain was now reunited with the empire.

Portchester must have played an important part in these events, possibly serving as the home port of the out-flanked rebel navy. At any event, when Constantius set about reorganizing the province he would have been faced with the problem of what to do with the hitherto hostile naval strongholds. At Portchester there is evidence of the demolition of internal buildings at about this time. A large pit had been dug and into it had been thrown the debris from the demolition of wattle and daub buildings, from which the re-usable materials such as nails, roof tiles and possibly timbers, had been removed. The extent of the demolition is difficult to define but it is not impossible that the fort was entirely cleared. The potential danger of these coastal strong-points can hardly have been overlooked by the new government. During the next forty years, however, Portchester was re-occupied. Infant burials together with trinkets of varying kinds attest the presence of women; cats abounded and rubbish, including masses of kitchen refuse, was spread out in heaps over the streets. The evidence is suggestive of an essentially civilian occupation, perhaps by squatters making use of the protective walls. An alternative explanation is that the community may have been deliberately planted by Constantius is an attempt to demilitarize the coastal forts.

Under the peace which followed the restoration of Britain, the territory of the Regni, along with the rest of the province, flourished. Many of the villas reached a standard of luxury far above that of the previous generations, town houses were rebuilt in masonry in Chichester and patronage was sufficiently substantial to support specialist schools of mosaicists. Other public works were probably put in hand at this time. That roads, which were largely the responsibility of the local authorities, were repaired is shown by a milestone found near Worthing, erected during the reign of Constantius I (307-37).[14] The period of peace and prosperity was, however, short-lived.

In 342 Britain was once more plunged into a crisis situation requiring the attention of the emperor Constans, who made a surprising dash to the island in mid-winter. Such an unusual decision is a measure of the seriousness of the situation, though the cause of his concern is unknown. While in Britain Constans may well have reorganized the defences of the province. It was at about this time that Portchester was brought back into a state of military readiness: the rubbish was tidied up, the internal roads were re-metalled and new internal buildings of timber were erected. It must have been at this time that the *Numerus Exploratorum* was moved in to garrison the fort.[15] The name of the unit is recorded in Chapter XXVIII of the *Notitia Dignitatum*, which lists the troops under the command of the Count of the Saxon Shore (the *comes litoris Saxonici*) — a new command which would seem to reflect an organizational structure set up, quite possibly as a result of Constans' visit, to deal with the recurring menace of raiders from the sea. Under the jurisdiction of the Count, nine coastal forts are listed between Portchester and Brancaster (on the Wash). Beside Portchester, one other, Pevensey, falls within the territory.

Fig. 10. The walls of the fort at Pevensey

Pevensey (*Anderidos*)[16] was the base of the *Numerus Abulcorum*, a detachment of Germanic troops who were to remain there for at least 25 years (fig. 10). The new fort was built at about the time of Constans' visit: large numbers of coins of the 340s have been discovered in excavation and a coin dating to 330-5 was found beneath one of the bastions. Together the evidence is suggestive of a construction date centring on about 340. The fort, while similar in basic concept to Portchester, embodied a number of improvements. Instead of adhering to the rigid formality of rectangular layout, the walls of Pevensey formed a roughly oval shape following the contour of the hillock upon which it stood (fig. 11). Its main west gate was an improvement on the Portchester gate type with the courtyard effect created by bringing the two adjacent bastions together and setting the guard chambers immediately inside, projecting into the fort. The east gate was a simple 10 ft. wide archway set in the wall with no guard chambers, while the north postern was designed to be a sinuous s-shaped passage built into the

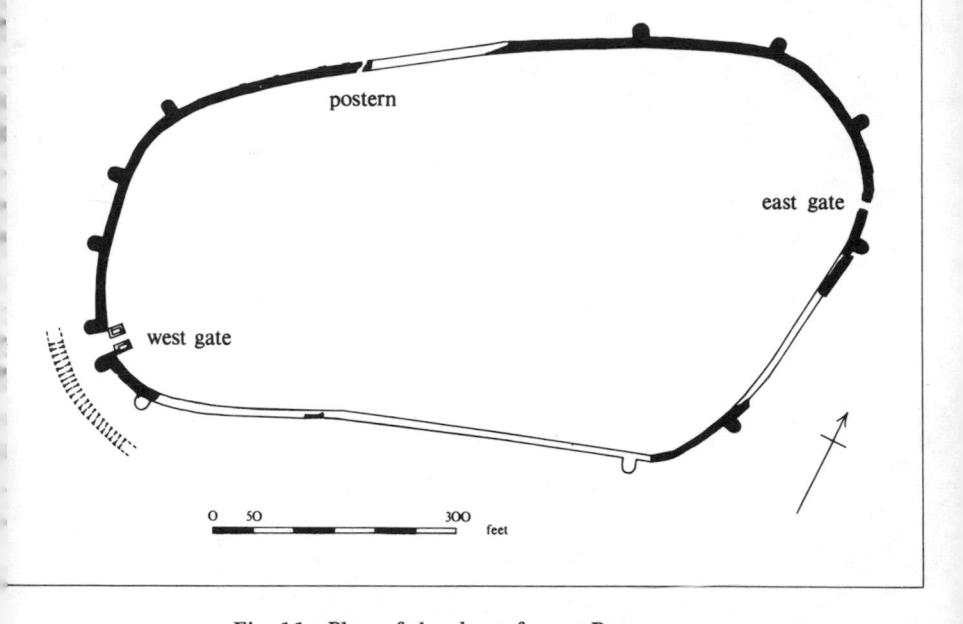

Fig. 11. Plan of the shore fort at Pevensey

thickness of the wall with evident defensive advantages.

It is in the arrangement of the forward-projecting bastions (fig. 12) that Pevensey shows its originality in breaking away from standard Roman practice. Instead of being spaced at regular intervals as they are at Portchester, each bastion is placed so as to be intervisible with its neighbours. Thus where the fort wall curves sharply they are close together, but along straight stretches a wider spacing is adopted. The design was concerned simply to eliminate dead ground; regularity was no longer demanded. Little is known of the internal arrangements of the fort but during the excavations of 1906-8 a series of regularly spaced hearths were found which suggest an ordered arrangement, perhaps belonging to the barrack buildings housing the troops. Together Portchester and Pevensey would have provided protection for the entire coastal region of the Regni – a protection which, as the second half of the fourth century approached, was very badly needed.

In 350 Magnentius made a bid for the throne. He appears to have had British connections and was supported by a large army raised in the province, but his defeat in 351 and death

Fig. 12. One of the bastions at Pevensey

two years later left Britain on the wrong side. The new emperor Constantius was not slow to extract his revenge from among the British aristocracy who had supported Magnentius. It was during this troubled time that a vast hoard of 1800 coins was hidden at Redford near Pulborough.[17] Another hoard of 2000 'folles' of the House of Constantine, discovered just beyond the western limit of the territory near Hamble, dates from about the same period.[18]

Britain found it difficult to recover. Short of manpower, still suffering from the reprisals and required to supply corn for Julian's army in Germany, the province trembled under a barbarian onslaught. The Scots from Ireland and the Picts from Scotland attacked the northern frontier in 360. Five years later Picts, Scots, Attacotti and Saxons attacked again with even more success. Thus the stage was set for the fiercest of all Barbarian invasions, the great 'Barbarian conspiracy' of 367, in which Hadrian's Wall was overrun while fully garrisoned and the province was disrupted to as far south as the Thames.

3.

Communications and urban settlement

The settlement pattern and the communications network in the territory of the Regni were determined to a considerable extent by the rigid and dominating structure of the landscape, which not only created natural lines of communication between one place and the next but also offered not inconsiderable obstacles to tax the ingenuity of the early Roman engineers.[1]

The Regni could boast only one urban centre, *Noviomagus*, which developed, or more correctly was created, close to the heart of the old pre-Roman kingdom in the centre of the fertile coastal plain. Much of its wealth and prosperity would have depended upon the continued exploitation of the rich farmlands which spread for miles both to the east and west between the Downs and the sea. *Noviomagus* was linked by main roads to the neighbouring urban centres (fig. 13). One road, Stane Street, crossed the Weald on a near direct route to London; another somewhat more torturous course led to Silchester, again cutting for many miles through the forests and heaths of the Weald; the third chose an easier route, first along the coastal plain, then picking out a sandy ridge and finally across the chalk Downs to Winchester. London was 56 miles away, Silchester 38 and Winchester 33.

The existence of the three main arteries was demanded by the presence of the towns and the administrative need to link them as directly as possible. The other roads were more a convenience providing cross-country routes between one place and another and offering rapid access between areas of high productive capacity and their nearest markets. The two trans-Wealden routes leading from the Brighton and Lewes areas respectively and converging on London may well have been constructed to link the corn-producing Downland and the iron-rich Weald direct to the capital (fig. 14). After all, by Roman road the east Sussex Downs were as near to London as they were to Chichester, and to have carted iron from the Weald to Chichester rather than London would have meant an extra half day's journey. In this simple observation may lie the reason why no major urban centre developed in east Sussex — the area was strictly within the economic hinterland of London.

Lateral routes also existed running east to west, following the grain of the land. The Bitterne-and-Winchester-to-Chichester road was continued eastwards to the Brighton area, its line carefully following the southern edge of the Downs, while parallel to it lay another road picking out the Upper greensand ridge along the Wealden edge in front of the Downland scarp slope. This northern route served to link the three trans-Wealden roads and in all probability continued west, beyond Stane Street, to Winchester. The line of this section has not, however, been established except for a short length of some 6 miles leading directly to the east gate of the town.

Within the basic skeleton of major roads lay many other routes. Some, like the road to Pevensey, apparently constructed on a basis of many short alignments, may well have been laid out late in the Roman period to link the naval base to the main network; Portchester may also have been served in this way, but the route has still to be traced. And below all this would have lain a network of minor trackways, many of them already hundreds of years old when the Romans arrived, running from farm to farm, joining to the ancient Downland tracks and eventually tying up with the major routes, so that even the remotest peasants could make use of the new marketing facilities of the neighbouring towns.

Apart from the roads themselves, little is known of the ancillary works connected with road construction. Only one milestone has been found, which was presumably derived from the south coast road but was subsequently carted to the site of a Roman building near West Worthing.[2] It refers to

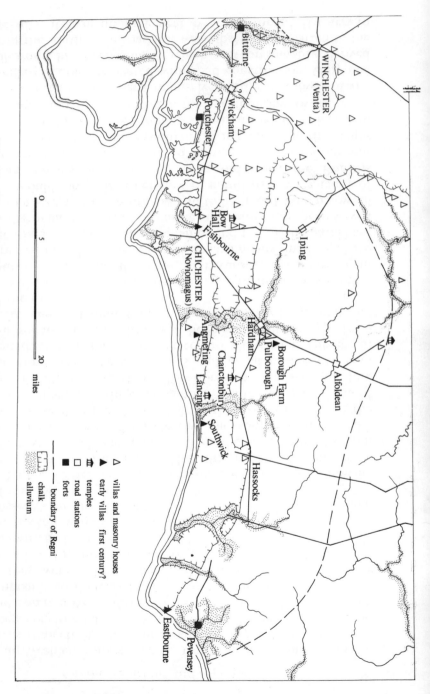

Fig. 13. Communications and settlement in the territory of the Regni

Legend:

△ villas and masonry houses
▲ early villas first century?
⊞ temples
□ road stations
■ forts
— boundary of Regni
▒ chalk alluvium

Map labels:

WINCHESTER (Venta)
Bitterne
Wickham
Porchester
Iping
Bow Hill
Fishbourne
CHICHESTER (Noviomagus)
Angmering
Hardham
Pulborough
Borough Farm
Alfoldean
Chanctonbury
Lancing
Southwick
Hassocks
Eastbourne
Pevensey

0 5 20 miles

Fig. 14. An exposed area of the Roman road from London to Lewis

Constantine I and is likely therefore to relate to some act of reconstruction work carried out early in the fourth century.

One obstacle facing the road builders would have been the crossing of the many rivers which dissect the territory. Where the rivers were, narrow bridges would have been built, like the simple timber structure which took Stane Street across the River Arun near Alfoldean.[3] The foundations were apparently based on abutments of stone and rubble, revetted by double rows of stakes, while the bridge itself was probably little more than a series of timbers laid horizontally between the abutments, perhaps with some kind of central support. Bridging operations of this kind would have posed little problem, but crossing the wide valleys of the Adur and Arun was far more difficult, not the least because of the width of their flood plains. We can only suppose that causeways were built out as far as possible and that ferries were provided between the terminals.

In addition to roads, the rivers and the sea would have provided an essential means of communication. The four major Sussex rivers slicing through the Downland ridge were navigable by barge and small boat from the sea right into the Weald. Supplies of iron, corn, stone or tiles could have been transported to Chichester far more rapidly and cheaply by boat than by road. Heavy commodities from further afield, like building stone from Bembridge in the Isle of Wight or the blue shelly marble from the Isle of Purbeck, almost certainly reached Chichester by sea.

The existence of coastal trade implies the presence of ports and other harbour installations. At Fishbourne, one mile west of Chichester, extensive wharfs and jetties have been found together with traces of dredging activities designed to provide deep water channels for boats.[4] Work began in the early 50s and the arrangements were maintained until the palace was constructed in *c.* 75, at which time the harbour built around the eastern arm of the inlet was converted for domestic and scenic use. The possibility remains that the western creek-end, which has not been examined archaeologically, may have continued to be used commercially, but the expansion of the Flavian palace must have cut off any direct links between the harbour and the town of Chichester. This does not, of course, preclude the development of port facilities further south along the Fishbourne creek, perhaps in the region of Dell Quay, which became the port of Chichester in medieval and later times, sited a little over a mile from the town.

Little is known of the other harbours which must have existed. The fourth-century fort at Pevensey would have been provided with docking arrangements for the fleet connected with Channel patrols. Similar installations presumably existed at Portchester. The naval base at Portchester was established on a virgin site, but the Pevensey fort was evidently preceded by earlier occupation which might well have been associated with the exploitation of the potentially valuable port facilities. Maritime links between east Sussex and Kent would have been far more efficient than journeys by road. The estuaries of the four rivers which cut through the Sussex Downs provide excellent harbours. Modern developments at Shoreham at the mouth of the Adur and Newhaven on the River Ouse demonstrate the potential of these sites today, but of their possible Roman predecessors there is no trace. One possibility is that, with less silting of the estuaries and shallower-draught boats, ports may have developed further inland. This, however, is speculative and cannot yet be verified.

Within this complex communications network several nucleations of population developed. Only one, *Noviomagus* (Chichester), can properly be called a town.[5] It inherited its urban tradition from the old native capital in the Selsey region, and under the patronage of Cogidubnus it rapidly developed as an administrative and market centre of some sophistication. Elsewhere smaller centres were initiated but they mostly failed to achieve urban status (pp. 69-73).

The tribal capital

Noviomagus, the capital of the Regni, lies beneath the present market town of Chichester on the Sussex coastal plain (fig. 15). The land hereabouts is flat, seldom exceeding 40-50 ft. OD, a characteristic determined by the nature of the sub-soil which here consists of a thick blanket of gravelly 'coombe rock' overlaid by, on average, 3 ft. of porous orange brickearth. The town was sited midway between Fishbourne Channel and the River Lavant which originally ran due south into Pagham harbour, but was later diverted (p. 56). Four approach roads are known or suspected: Stane Street running from the east gate to London with a branch road serving the coastal plain converging about 1½ miles from the town; a road to Bitterne (*Clausentum*) from the west gate; a road to Silchester (*Calleva*) from the north gate, while a road towards Selsey in all probability ran southwards from the south gate. There may also have been a number of minor roads and tracks converging on the town like the long stretch of straight road which ran from the Downs, in the area of West Stoke, towards the north gate. With the exception of the building at Fishbourne, one mile to the west of the town, no villas are

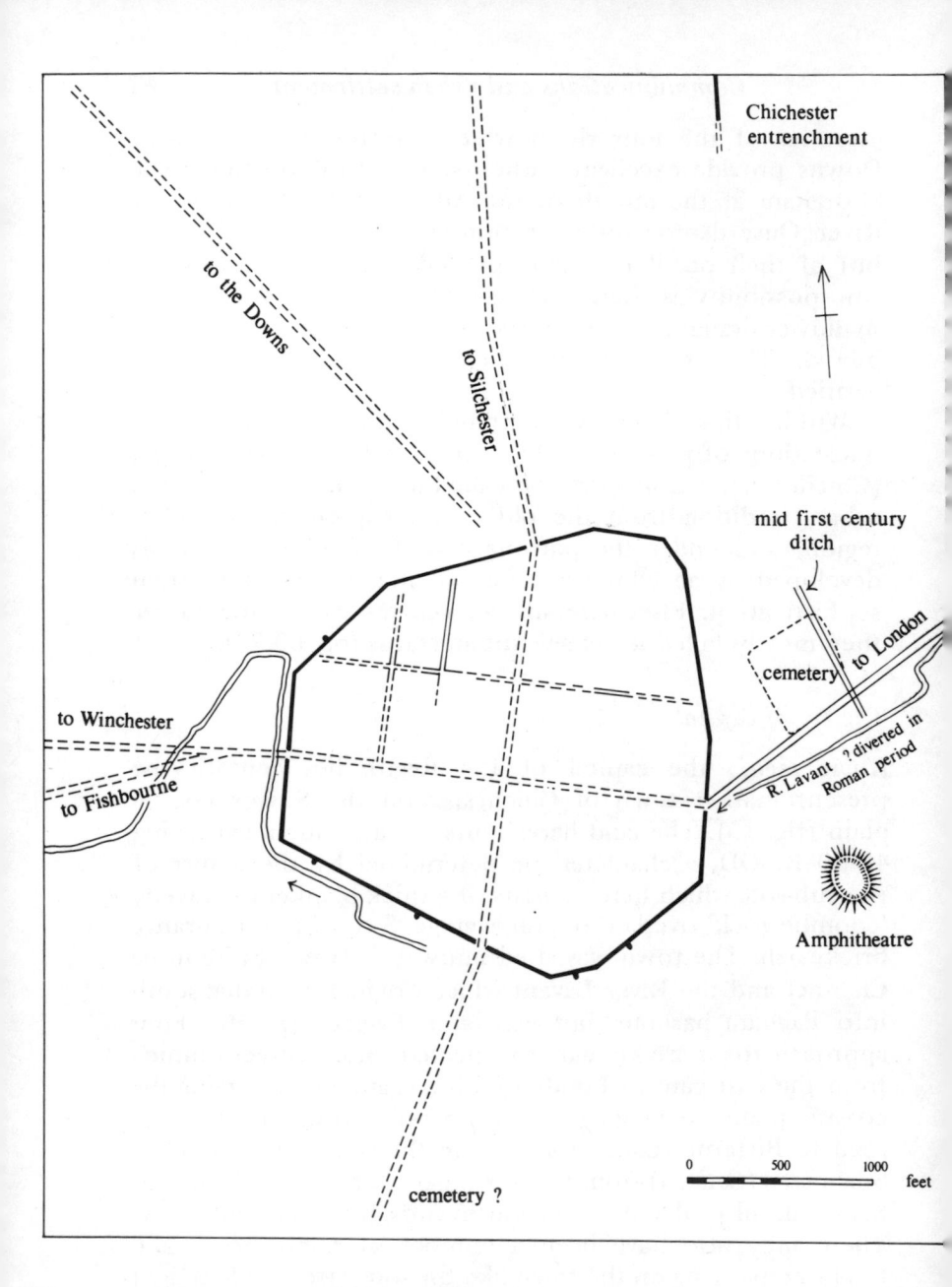

Fig. 15. Chichester and its environs

known within a three-mile radius of the centre. The area may perhaps represent the *territorium* of the town, the land being worked directly by the inhabitants.

The name of the town, given by Ptolemy as *Noviomagus* and repeated as *Navimago* in the Ravenna cosmography, is relatively common in the Roman world. It is generally taken to mean the 'new plain' or 'new field': in other words a clearing. Such a description would be appropriate to a new foundation established on an open site at the beginning of the Roman period.[6] The apparent absence of pre-Roman occupation material beneath Chichester would tend to support this view. While too much weight should not be placed on mere absence of evidence, on the present showing it may tentatively be assumed that *Noviomagus* originated as a Roman establishment, possibly as the direct result of official encouragement to the population to leave the native capital in the region of Selsey and settle around the new location (pp. 16-17).

The context of a military presence at Chichester in the early years of the Roman occupation has already been discussed in broad historical terms (pp. 24-7). The growing archaeological data hardly allows such a presence to be doubted. The most dramatic evidence comes in the form of a large number of articles of military equipment found in various parts of the town (fig. 16). A collection made before the war from the area of Little London,[7] in the north-east quarter, includes a fine legionary belt-plate, a belt or apron-plate, a buckle, a cuirass hook and a silvered belt-end – all apparently from the excavation of a limited area. Nearby another cuirass hook and a harness buckle were found in the excavations of 1959-64. More recently a wide range of military bronzes have been recovered from the excavation in Chapel Street from levels of pre-Flavian date. Outstanding among the finds was an exquisitely decorated belt-plate (fig. 16); other items include belt buckles, lorica plates, cuirass hinges, a plume mount, phalerae and scabbard bindings.[8] There can be very little doubt therefore that a military detachment, including, at the very least, a proportion of legionary troops, was stationed at some stage on the site of the town.

Structural evidence which might be considered to be of military origin is now beginning to accumulate. Outside the east gate of the town, beneath the cremation cemetery at St. Pancras, a length of ditch has come to light measuring some 10 ft. wide and 5 ft. deep, with a flat bottom.[9] Alongside, and running parallel, lay a slighter gully which might have supported a palisade, but the evidence is inconclusive. The finds from the ditch were all pre-Flavian. If it were thought to be a defensive ditch of military origin, and if the 'palisade' was contemporary, the fort would have to lie to the east, that is away from the town. If the 'palisade' was not relevant, the fort could lie to the west, but even a fortress of legionary size could not have been so large as to incorporate the areas where the military bronzes were discovered. On the present showing, therefore, it is simpler to assume that the military establishment lies beneath the town and that the St. Pancras ditch may belong to the beginning of the civilian phase (p. 53).

The most extensive areas to be excavated within the town lie along the west side of Chapel Street. Here a complex of timber buildings have been discovered, the earliest phases of which may well prove to be of military origin. Elsewhere occupation layers and drainage gulleys of pre-Flavian date may eventually be interpreted as belonging to the military phase when more is known of the overall plan of the earliest levels.

The military presence is unlikely to have lasted long — three or four years at the very most (p. 26); thereafter civilian control began. The early stages of urban development can most clearly be seen in the Chapel Street excavations,[10] where after the supposed military phase a new series of timber buildings were erected over the destroyed daub walls of the early structures. Later, probably early in the Neronian period, one area was developed as a pottery work-shop. Two kilns, together with their puddling pits, have been excavated. Both kilns were of updraught type; one of them, provided with two flues, had a firing chamber lined with small bricks laid horizontally in clay. Judging by the quantity of wasters lying about, the kilns specialized in the manufacture of white-ware beakers in the Gallo-Belgic style together with

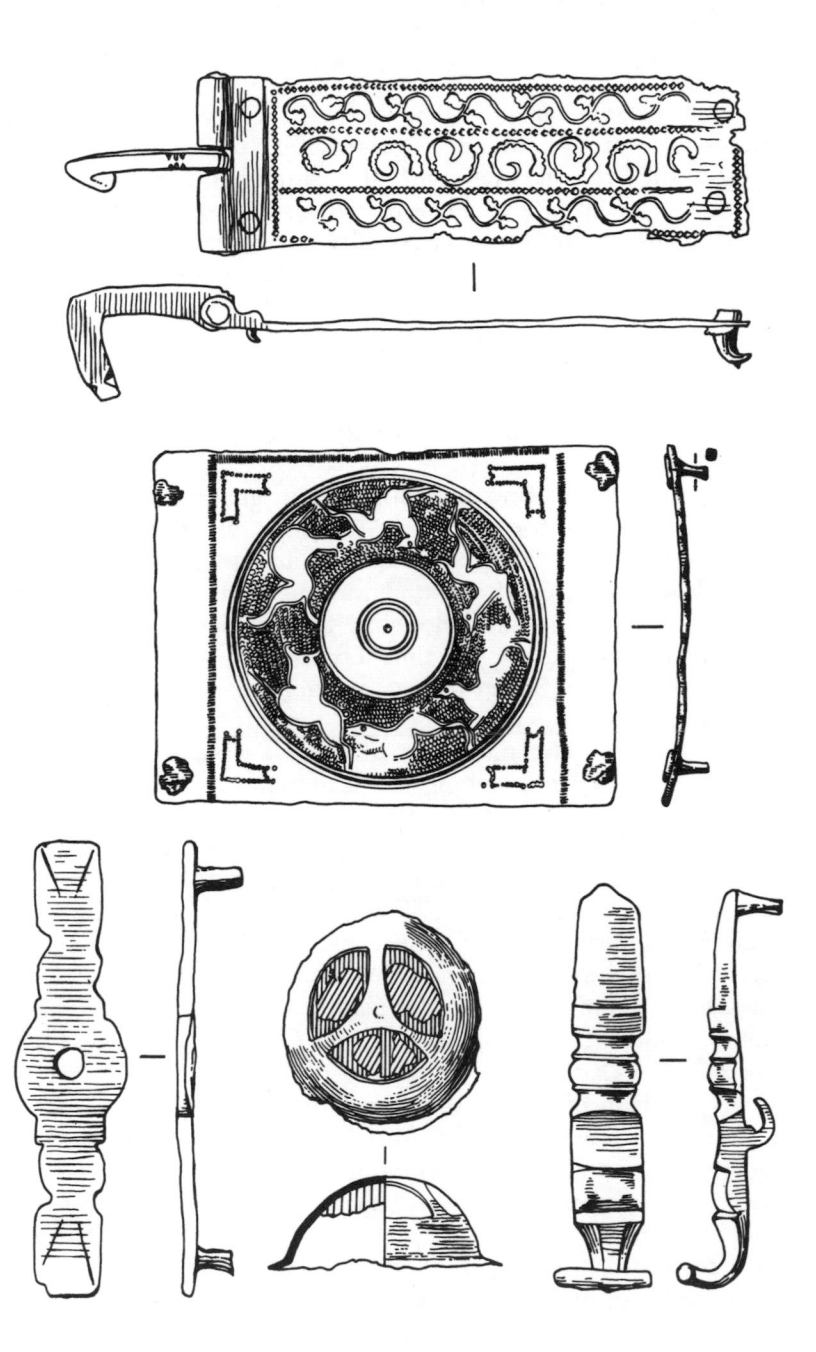

Fig. 16. Military bronzes from Chichester (1:1)

fine burnished carinated bowls and a range of coarser
domestic wares. The kilns can best be interpreted as
representing the development of a small industrial concern
geared to satisfying the more sophisticated needs of the
growing urban community. An alternative explanation, that
the kilns served a military market, seems less likely since it
would require the survival of the military presence probably
as late as the early 50s of the first century. This could, of
course, be justified if it is supposed that a small peace-
keeping detachment remained to safeguard the interests of
Cogidubnus, but evidence for or against such a view is totally
lacking.

After the kilns were abandoned, the ground was levelled
up and a new series of timber buildings erected, based on
horizontal timber sill beams laid on footings of stone and
flint. Several houses of this type have been found in different
parts of the town, all belonging to the Neronian or early
Flavian period. During this time a bronze works was set up in
one of the Chapel Street houses, the activity represented now
by hundreds of crucible fragments, together with droplets of
spilled bronze. The discovery of several pieces of glass frit
may suggest that enamelling was also being carried out in the
same workshop.

These well-constructed houses and the development of
workshop activity is indicative of the growth of urban life,
possibly under the paternal guidance of Cogidubnus. A
dramatic reminder of the sophistication of the community is
given by an inscription (now lost) found on the corner of
East Street and St. Martin's Lane in 1740.[11] It read: 'To
Nero Claudius, son of the divine Claudius, grandson of
Germanicus Caesar, great-grandson of Tiberius Caesar, great-
great-grandson of the divine Augustus, Caesar Augustus with
Tribunician power for the fourth time, Imperator for the
fourth time, Consul for the fourth time.' Allowing for an
error in the stone carving, requiring the emendation of the
consular years from IV to III, the inscription can be shown to
date to A.D. 58. Whether it served as a dedicatory inscription
for a building or for a statue of the emperor is uncertain, but
its very existence is an indication of a surprising degree of
civic awareness at an early stage in the town's development.

It remains a possibility that the Neronian town was defined by earthworks enclosing the urban area. If the ditch found beneath the St. Pancras cemetery is not military, it may prove to be an eastern boundary for the town at this stage in its development. A length of first-century ditch found to coincide approximately with the later south wall during the excavation of the Palace bastion possibly belongs to the same system, but this must remain in the realms of speculation until further work has been carried out. All that can safely be said is that the existence of a Neronian defensive circuit is a reasonable hypothesis.

The construction of the street grid cannot be dated with accuracy, but it is tolerably certain that most of the insulae were laid out by, or during, the Flavian era. To this period belongs a considerable expanse of gravel metalling up to 3 ft. thick, which has been sectioned on several sites in the centre of the town.[12] In extent, the gravel spreads 500 ft. north from West Street and from the area of Chapel Street for a distance of at least 150 ft. to the west. Most sections have shown that it consists of two distinct metallings separated by a very thin lens of soil, sand or sometimes, at the northern extremity, greensand chippings, thus representing two phases of deposition. There is, however, no reason to suppose a time-lag between the phases, since the evidence would allow that one phase followed rapidly upon the other as part of the same construction process. The simplest explanation for the gravelling is that it represents the construction of the forum, but until the surrounding building ranges have been defined it would be unwise to be too dogmatic, since the alternative view, that the gravelling was merely a general preliminary levelling, may eventually prove to be correct.

If, however, the gravel layers are the forum metalling, it is tempting to speculate as to the position of the basilica. The most likely site for it is along the south side of the metalling and fronting on to West Street. Two fragments of masonry may be relevant here: a massive 6 ft. wide wall of flints and mortar found beneath the frontage of the Dolphin Hotel in 1940, and a stone and mortar pier-base of substantial proportions seen in 1967 during the redevelopment of Nos. 3-5 North Street.[13] To attempt to reconstruct a basilica from so little is, to say the least, ill-advised but the masonry is massive enough to be regarded as belonging to an impressive public building, while the base *could* have supported one of the piers of the basilica arcades. Several architectural fragments which may have come from the basilica were found re-used beneath the cathedral on the opposite side of West Street. These included the base of a massive column, measuring 29 ins. in diameter, and at least four gutter blocks of the kind used in front of a stylobate.[14] The proportions of these pieces are such that they must have come from a public building of some magnitude, but not necessarily from the basilica. Thus it must be admitted that while a circumstantial case can be made out for the siting of the basilica, the evidence is still insufficient to offer any certainty.

The most significant discovery relating to the development of the town in the first century is the famous 'Cogidubnus stone', an inscription carved on a single slab of Purbeck marble once 5 ft. 3 ins. long by 2 ft. 7 ins. high.[15] The text reads:

> N] E P T V N O E T M I N E R V A E
> T E M P L V M
> PR]O   SALVTE   DO[MVS]   DIVINAE
> EX]   AVCTORITA[TE   TI.]CLAVD.
> CO]GIDVBINI R.L[EGA]T.AVG.IN BRIT.
> COLLE]GIVM FABROR. ET QVI IN E[O
> SVNT] D . S . D . DONANTE AREAM
> [CLEM]ENTE   PVDENTINI   FIL.

Clearly it is the dedicatory inscription from a temple of Neptune and Minerva erected for the well-being of the Divine household of the emperor (*pro salute domus divinae*). The temple was paid for by a guild of craftsmen (*collegium fabrorum*) and put up on a site given by one Clemens son of Pudentinus, the whole operation being undertaken with the permission (*ex auctoritate*) of king Tiberius Claudius Cogidubnus, Imperial legate in Britain (*legati augusti in Britannia*). Herein lies a fascinating insight into the degree of Romanization experienced by the early town: the emperor's family was being honoured, Roman gods were worshipped and artisans were organized into guilds in the Roman manner. Moreover, they were able to employ craftsmen of considerable skill to carve the dedication and, no doubt, to erect and decorate the building. The inscription was found face downwards in 1723 during building operations on a site fronting North Street, close to the junction with Lion Street. Since it is unlikely to have been moved far from its place of display, it may reasonably be assumed that the temple occupied a prominent position, quite possibly at the junction of two Roman streets (fig. 17). When it was erected is a matter for debate, but reasons have been given (pp. 26-7) for supposing the inscription to belong to the early 70s. It is therefore tempting to see the temple as one of the public buildings put up early in the Flavian period when the town seems to have undergone a phase of rapid development and aggrandizement.

Another public building which seems to have been constructed in the Flavian period is the amphitheatre, which lay on the western edge of the city.[16] Relatively limited excavation has shown the arena to measure 185 ft. by 150 ft., comparable in proportions and size to the amphitheatre at Caerleon. It would appear that the structure was short-lived since there is some evidence to suggest the robbing of its masonry towards the end of the second century.

A town the size of Chichester must have been provided with a suite of public baths, together with the ancilliary engineering works required both to supply the necessary fresh water and to drain away waste. The site of the baths probably lay to the west of the gravelled area of the 'forum' where, in 1962, part of a massive apse built of flint and stone was discovered during building work.[17] The depth of the pink mortar floor of the apse, some 10-11 ft. below the modern surface, strongly suggests that it was, in fact, the basement floor of a hypocaust which has since been destroyed. A small fragment of mosaic pavement found some 40 ft. away may be part of the same building. While it is possible that the apse belongs to a private house, the massive nature of its masonry is strongly suggestive of a public building.

The water supply for the baths, and indeed for the town in

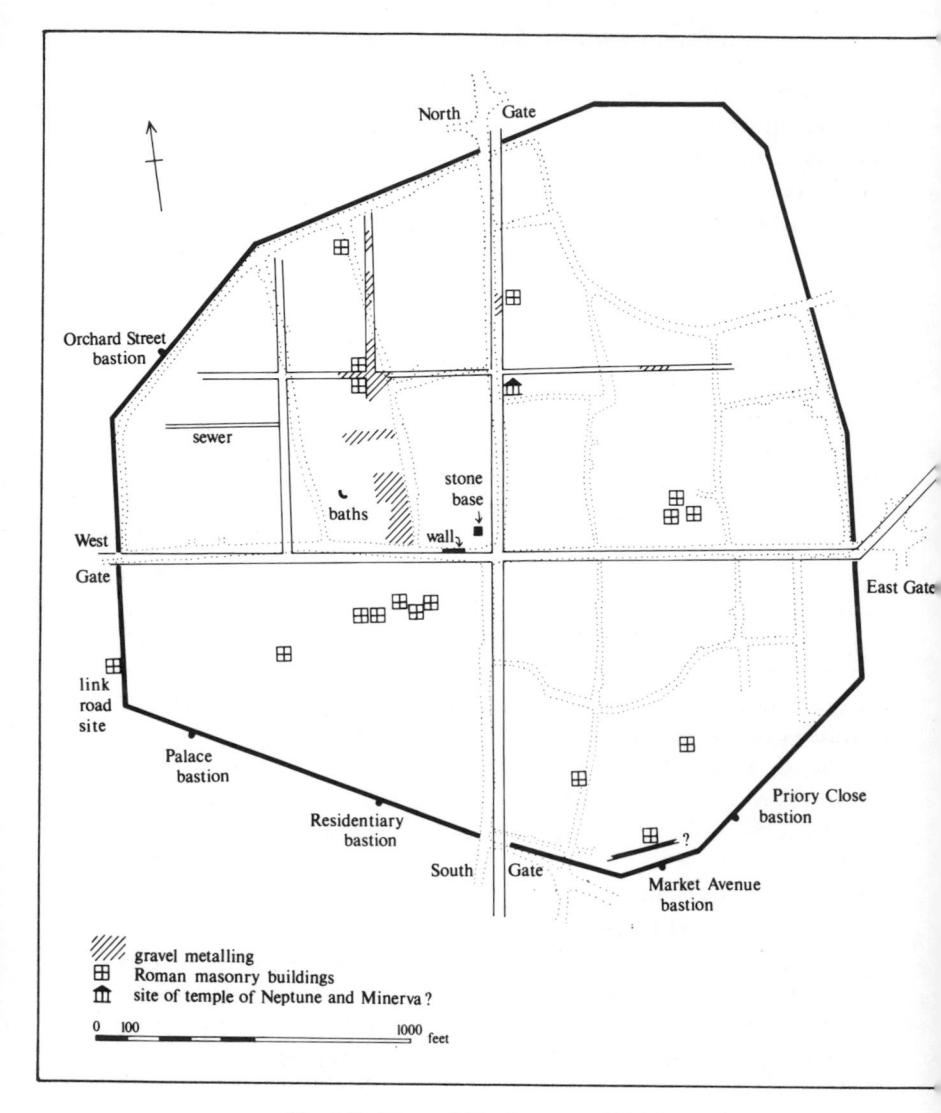

Fig. 17. Plan of *Noviomagus* (Chichester)

general, was tapped from the River Lavant which would originally have crossed the line of Stane Street a little under a mile from the town. At some stage the river was diverted along the Roman road towards the town and now runs in a loop around the southern side of the walled area to join with a stream flowing into Fishbourne channel. The date of the diversion is unknown, but probably took place early in the Roman period to serve the increasing needs of the community. Not all of the private houses would have used the public supply. The second-century house now beneath the link road close to the west wall of the town was provided with its own stone-lined well tapping one of the copious springs only a few feet below the surface. Many of the individual houses would have been supplied in this way.

Some evidence for the drainage system has recently come to light beneath and adjacent to the County Hall.[18] Here a substantial timber-lined sewer, originally some 2 ft. wide and 6 ft. deep, has been traced for a distance of 250 ft., no doubt draining the central area and possibly the baths, by channelling the waste water out of the town and into the streams beyond the west wall. No close dating evidence survives for the construction of the system, but it had ceased to function by the late fourth or early fifth century, by which time it had become choked with occupation rubbish.

Throughout the second century the town spread outwards unhindered, except perhaps by the lines of any first-century defences or boundary which might have survived. At the end of the century, however, the urban nucleus was formally defined by the construction of an encircling bank and ditch enclosing an area of about 100 acres.[19] The bank was some 25 or 30 ft. wide and up to 10 ft. high, and in front of it were two V-shaped ditches from which much of the gravel and clay of the bank must have been derived. The pottery stratified within and beneath the earthwork suggests that the construction must date to the end of the second century at the very earliest.

At a later date, probably early in the third century, the front of the earthwork was cut back and a wall some 6 or 7 ft. thick was added to revet the face of the bank, while its height was increased by the addition of further layers of gravel and clay, so that it now formed a backing rampart of the wall (fig. 18). This relationship between the wall and the bank has now been established at several points, at Crawley Priory and the Palace bastion sites on the south wall and at the West Gate and Orchard Street in the west and north sectors. It is therefore reasonably certain that the wall closely

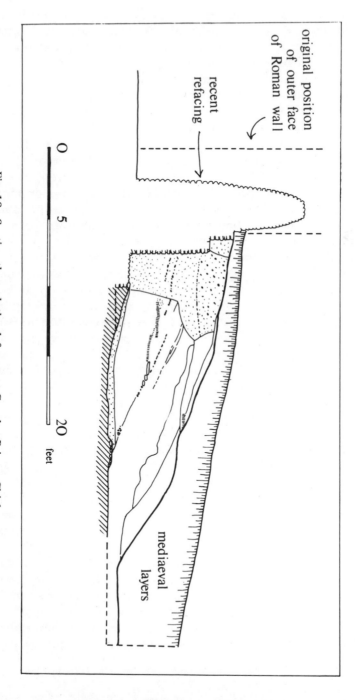

original position
of outer face
of Roman wall

recent
refacing

mediaeval
layers

0   5   20 feet

Fig. 18. Section through the defences at Crawley Priory, Chichester

followed the bank around the entire circuit. The wall itself was built of courses of flints set between thick bands of mortar. Although it still survives for almost its entire length, the original facing has everywhere been replaced on more than one occasion by medieval and later repairs. At Priory Close, however, part of the original facing survived, protected by the mass of a later bastion added some time towards the end of the fourth century. Here the wall was found to be faced with a neat ashlar of small greensand blocks set in courses and pointed with a hard red mortar. It may well be that the entire external face was originally treated in this way.

Little is know of the form of the Roman gates. A woodcut by Grimm, which shows the West Gate at the end of the eighteenth century, suggests that a substantial part of the Roman structure was still surviving at this time, but the point is at present impossible to prove since the site of the foundations lies beneath a modern road junction.[20] Some part of the Roman North Gate was, however, exposed in 1950 when a petrol tank was constructed. The surviving remains consisted of a massive stone block possibly forming the south-east corner of the gate tower to which, apparently, the city wall had been abutted.[21] If this is so, it raises the possibility that the gates may have been built together with the earthwork before the wall was added — a sequence of events which has been suggested for a number of other towns in southern Britain. Of the other entrances nothing is yet known; the east gate is likely to be beneath the present road but more uncertainty attaches to the position of the south gate. If the alignment of the north-south street suggested here (fig. 17) is correct, the gate must lie to the east of the present road, but limited rescue excavation on the site has so far failed to trace it.

The encircling of the urban nucleus first with a bank and soon afterwards with a wall is a phenomenon common to a number of towns, particularly in the south-east of Britain. Various explanations for this have been put forward, but since they mostly depend upon correlations with historical events, and since close dating for the building work is seldom available, there can be little certainty as to the true causes.[22]

The most plausible explanation, however, is that the earth-work defences (together with the masonry gates, if they prove to be contemporary) were put up some time after 196, the year in which the Governor of Britain, Clodius Albinus, stripped the province of troops in support of his campaign for the crown. News of the event must have been widespread, not the least after the Barbarians had broken through Hadrian's Wall, with the depletion of its garrisons. At such a time as this some defensive measures would not have been out of place.

The addition of city walls may have come either soon afterwards as part of the same process or a decade or two later; it is at present difficult to demonstrate the length of time-gap between the two works. Another possible context, either for the addition of the wall, or for both earthworks and wall if they are considered to be of roughly the same date, is the year 212 A.D. when Caracalla gave all free-born inhabitants of towns the right of Roman citizenship. Such a momentous step in urban development is unlikely to have gone unmarked. The formal definition of the city bounds would have been an appropriate act to symbolize the event.

At Chichester, as elsewhere, the line taken by the defences did not include the entire built-up area — the fringes were omitted. This was very clearly demonstrated at the link road site, just outside the west wall, where the remains of a masonry building and what may be a section of a street were sliced across by the defences.[23] In fact on all sides of the town Roman occupation levels of the first and second centuries have come to light beyond the walls. The degree of shrinkage represented by the wall building can only be defined when the full extent of the early settlement has been traced and its defences, if any, have been located.

Relatively little is known of the appearance of the town in the third and fourth centuries. Most of the public buildings would have been maintained, with the exception of the amphitheatre, which appears to have been demolished by this time. A reminder that monumental works were being undertaken in the late second or early third century is however given by a sculptured block found in the 'forum' area when the Post Office was being built on the corner of

West Street and Chapel Street.[24] The stone is evidently part of a free-standing pedestal base, probably for a Jupiter column, since one face bears the inscription:

I O M
IN HONOREM DO
MV[S] DIVINA...

'To Jupiter, the greatest of the gods, in honour of the Divine House...'

The other side of the block is carved with a shallow recess containing two naked female figures against a background of foliage: of the other two sides little can be seen except for an arm of a figure holding a sceptre of spear, which could be Jupiter himself, on one face, and a fragment of foliage on the other. That all four sides were sculptured or inscribed shows that the block must have stood free. Allowing for a base and a top moulding, it would originally have been about 4 ft. high supporting a column, probably in excess of 20 or 30 ft., surmounted by a statue of the god. Sited somewhere in the forum it must have formed an imposing monument, adding considerably to the dignity of the city.

Other inscriptions are rare in Chichester, but mention should be made of an altar found in 1823 under the pavement in front of a house next to the Little London Inn in North Street, not far from the Cross.[25] It was inscribed:

GENIO S
LVCVLLVS
AMMINI. FIL
D S P

'Sacred to the Genius of this place, Lucullus, son of Amminius, set this up from his own resources.'

It clearly derives from a religious place, perhaps a temple, somewhere in the city, but there is no reason to suppose that the site lay in North Street where the stone was found, since it may well have been moved around and re-used after the Roman period. Nevertheless it is a further indication of the religious life of the community.

About the middle of the second century many of the privately owned houses within the town began to be rebuilt in masonry. Something of this development is shown by the area on either side of the east-west street at its junction with the Roman predecessor of Chapel Street.[26] Here, current excavations have defined a series of rebuilding phases, during which the houses or shops gradually encroached upon the streets. One of them was provided with a small hypocaust, the other with a tesselated floor. Both seem to have been U-shaped in plan with three ranges laid out about a central courtyard.

The Chapel Street complex is the largest area to be thoroughly excavated within the Roman town: elsewhere only fragments of buildings have come to light, often multilated by medieval and later disturbances. At North Street (St. Peter-the-Less) three rooms were examined belonging to a substantial house fronting on to the main street.[27] Even in this central position it would appear that the site continued to be occupied by timber structures until masonry replacement was undertaken in the late third or early fourth century. An earlier, and rather more substantial, town house has been examined from time to time below the cathedral, where the discovery of tesselated floors, a hypocaust and a fragment of a polychrome mosaic floor all point to a building of some quality.[28] The mosaic, though fragmentary, is an accomplished piece of work incorporating a rosette contained within a square guilloche frame, the whole being linked to similar motifs by a simple Greek key pattern. Another town house was found in the same part of the city in 1725-7 during the rebuilding of part of the Bishop's Palace. Several rooms are said to have been uncovered, one of which contained the substantial part of a mosaic pavement. The eastern area of the town has also produced evidence of houses of quality. One found behind No. 30 East Street, evidently possessed a private bath suite, one room of which was floored with a polychrome mosaic.[29] The houses may have extended beneath St. Andrew's Church, where the presence of a tesselated pavement is recorded.

Although other structural remains have turned up from

time to time within the city, there is too little to allow much to be said of urban growth or planning. Nevertheless the general impression given is that throughout the Roman period large areas of the town were left open, the richer houses clustering along the main streets. It might even be thought that Chichester did not share in the spate of fourth-century rebuilding and aggrandizement apparent in other Romano-British towns.

Chichester was provided with two main cemeteries, one outside the East Gate along Stane Street, the other beyond the South Gate. The Eastern cemetery, called after the medieval burial ground of St. Pancras which later occupied part of the Roman site, has been known since 1895 when some 150 pots belonging to cremation burials were recovered by Councillor Butler, excavating beneath the floors of a row of cottages. More extensive excavations undertaken between 1934 and 1937, following the demolition of the cottages, brought to light 65 burial groups,[30] and when the site was cleared once more in 1965 an even larger scale excavation was mounted, increasing the total of stratified burials to 326.[31] Trial excavations have established that the cemetery occupied about 4.3 acres on the north side of Stane Street. Working from the known density of about 2,300 burials per acre, the total cemetery population is likely to have been of the order of 10,000. With the exception of 9 scattered inhumations, all the burials were cremations, displaying a considerable range of burial ritual. More than half of the graves were furnished with single cremation urns which normally, though not invariably, contained the cremated bones. In only two examples of this category were any rich grave goods buried. One was provided with a tinned bronze mirror in a leather case, together with a bracelet and a needle; while another, also presumably a woman, contained a ring and brooch. The other 144 were without signs of elaboration or wealth. The second type of burial, which amounted to about 44% of the total, were all furnished with ritual meals represented by accessory vessels including plates, flagons, cups and sometimes shale plates, eating utensils and joints of meat (fig. 19). These richer burials often contained personal belongings such as jewellery, mirrors, tools, games, boots and lamps, reflecting a belief in the afterlife. The same belief is also demonstrated by the provision of a coin with some of the dead to pay for the journey to the other world. In one grave the interred ashes were linked to the outside world by a pipe made of two imbrex tiles placed together so that libations to the dead man could be passed down to him.

Of these richer burials more than half were laid out with little apparent design in shallow pits, but the remainder were carefully arranged, some with the accessory vessels placed in a crescent, others with all vessels and grave goods contained within a wooden box or tile-built cist. This type of cist burial remained popular among the Regni throughout the first to third centuries, particularly in the Chichester region.

The careful excavation and analysis of part of the St. Pancras cemetery has provided a clear insight into the beliefs and rituals of the Roman population of Chichester. The dating evidence shows that burial at this spot began *c.*70-80 and continued until the late third century, by which time the rite was changing from cremation to inhumation. Since much of the central and western part of the cemetery lies beneath the medieval burial ground and is thus largely destroyed or unavailable for excavation, the full history of the Roman cemetery is unlikely to be discovered, but limited trial work has suggested that the pre-Flavian nucleus may lie further west. The relative lack of fourth-century inhumations on the excavated site need not imply that burial had ceased by the early fourth century: it may well be that the nucleus of the inhumation cemetery lies somewhere beneath the medieval grave-yard, but untangling skeletons of the two periods would be an extremely difficult task.

Of the southern cemetery very little is known, but cremation and inhumation burials were recorded in 1819 when the canal basin was being dug, and two tombstones found near the site of south gate in 1833 may also have derived from this burial ground.[32] Both are now very battered, but they may be read as follows:

]CCA AELIA/ . . .] CAUUA/ . . . .]
FIL(IA) AN(NORUM) XXXVI

'. . .cca . . .Aelia . . .Cauva, daughter of . . . aged 36.'

Fig. 19. A grave in the St. Pancras cemetery, Chichester

'CATIA . . ./CENSORIN[I . . . ./AN(NORUM) XXIII[. . . .

'Catia . . .of Censorinus, aged 23 [or 24].'

A third tombstone[33] found somewhere in the south-east part of the town in 1809 records the death of an old man at the age of 85. These three mutilated gravestones are a disappointingly meagre sample from what may once have been the principal upper-class cemetery of the town.

Before leaving the Chichester burial grounds, something must be said of a group of rich cist-burials found in the neighbourhood of the town at Westergate, Avisford, Aldingbourne and Densworth.[34] The Densworth site was apparently a cemetery of some size, where at least five interments were made. Two were set within stone-walled enclosures, one of which produced, in addition to its tile-built cist, fragments of a Purbeck marble inscription. Nearby was a stone cist containing a glass cremation jar with the ashes of a child inside, together with three other glass vessels and a pair of sandals. At Avisford, near Walberton, a similar stone-built cist was discovered containing the glass cremation bottle, a pair of sandals, three jugs, two dishes standing in platters, nine

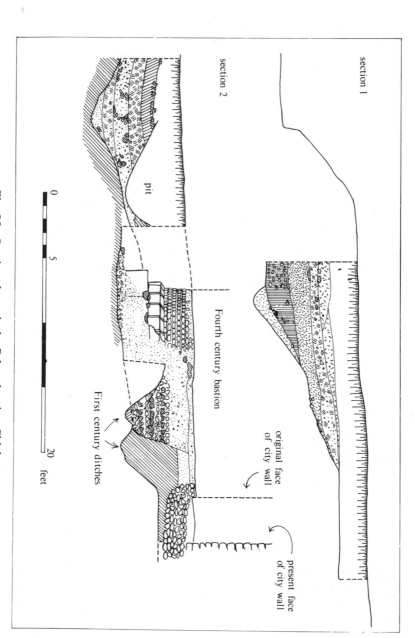

section 1

section 2

pit

Fourth century bastion

First century ditches

original face
of city wall

present face
of city wall

0 5 20
feet

Fig. 20. Section through the Palace bastion Chichester

cups, two candle-holders and a two-handled globular glass vessel. The cist was provided with two brackets, each supporting a pottery lamp. The Aldingbourne cist differed slightly in that it retained traces of a gilded wooden lining. Inside, in addition to the cremation bottle, were two glass jars, each containing the remains of a scented fatty substance, probably a cosmetic.

The ritual practices and beliefs involved are clearly much the same as those reflected in the somewhat poorer graves of the broadly contemporary St. Pancras cemetery. These scattered rich burials presumably represent the private cemeteries of the local aristocracy. The apparent absence of villas in the neighbourhood of all of them raises the possibility that those interred may have been the urban rich who chose to be buried on their estates rather than in the town burial ground. It may be, however, that their villas lie nearby, still undiscovered.

Towards the end of the fourth century, possibly as a response to the political and military upsets of 367-9 (pp. 126-7), the walls of the town were put into a new defensive readiness. This was accomplished by the addition of massive forward-projecting D-shaped bastions to the face of the town wall, which neccessitated the filling-in of the inner ditch and the re-digging of the outer in a wide flat-bottomed form (fig. 20).[35] Functionally, one must suppose that the bastions supported defensive artillery, while the ditch kept any would-be attackers within maximum killing range. Such an arrangement has been recognized at a number of towns in Britain and must represent a widespread response to political troubles which now required the towns to turn themselves into defended strongholds.

At Chichester five bastions still survive, of which three have been examined by excavation within recent years. Originally each facet of the wall circuit would have been provided with at least one bastion, while the longer stretches, like the south wall, will have required more than one to provide the flanking fire necessary to make the system effective and to ensure that the approaches to the city were adequately protected. The superstructure of each bastion consisted of a rubble core faced with greensand blocks and pointed with pink mortar, built on a rectangular foundation of massive sandstone blocks. Quantities of re-used masonry were incorporated in the work, including a cornice moulding of monumental proportions found at the base of the Palace bastion and a column and a very weathered tombstone from the bastion in Friary Close. No doubt by the time that the bastions were erected, in the late fourth century, a number of buildings as well as old cemeteries were in ruins and were available to be used as quarries for building material.

The new defensive architecture suggests that the town may now have been defended by a garrison or at least by a militia on call to man the walls should the need arise. The only possible evidence for this from Chichester is a belt buckle of Germanic type found on the site of the County Hall. These buckles are generally thought to have been introduced in the late fourth and early fifth centuries by Germanic mercenaries employed to defend the forts and towns against Barbarian attack.[36] While too much weight should not be given to the isolated example from Chichester, it is tempting to see it as representing a new military presence which probably lasted well into the fifth century.

How the town itself fared throughout the last years of Roman rule is difficult to define. Many of the buildings must have continued in use until after the official abandonment of the province in 410. The only archaeological evidence at present available, from the Chapel Street site, shows a considerable decline in the standard of living in the two houses flanking the Roman cross-roads: in one house a succession of rough tile-built hearths were laid, while in the other post-holes and an oven were cut through a tesselated floor. This does not, however, imply universal decline: it may merely represent a change in function of the two houses concerned. Perhaps the peripheral areas were abandoned to mundane purposes while urban life continued to flourish along the main streets. These problems, and indeed the whole question of the nature of the sub-Roman occupation await the results of future excavations.

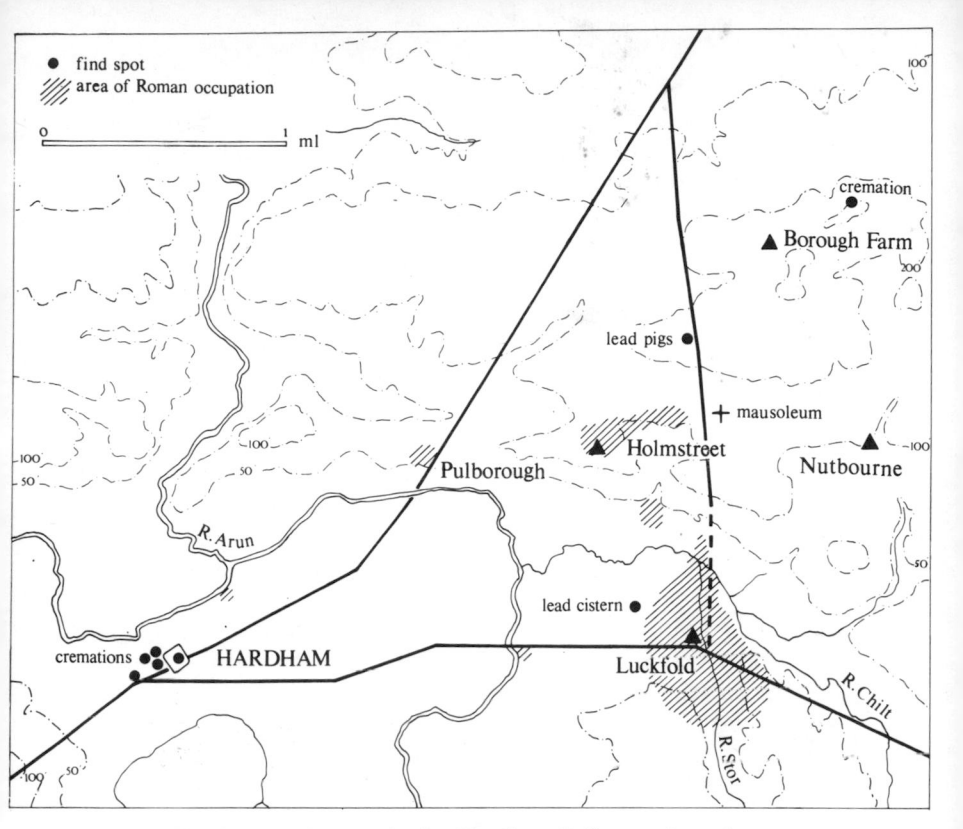

Fig. 21. Settlement in the Hardham-Pulborough region

Minor urban settlements

Besides the capital of Chichester several minor settlements
existed within the territory of the Regni, but for all of them
the evidence is unfortunately somewhat sparse. One of these,
Hardham, lies on the south bank of the River Arun astride
the line of Stane Street, about a mile and a half south of the
bridge which must have approximated to the ancient river
crossing (fig. 21). The site, now much mutilated by a railway line
and a disused gravel pit, originally consisted of a rectangular
earthwork enclosing some 4 acres. The only archaeological
work to be carried out, apart from casual observation and
collection in 1863 and again between 1898 and 1899, was a
limited excavation undertaken by Winbolt in 1926.[37] The
general result of this exploration suggests that the enclosure
was probably occupied from Neronian times until the middle
of the second century, after which part of it at least was used

as a cemetery, represented by a group of cremation burials.

That pottery manufacture was carried out nearby was suggested by a mass of early second-century wasters thrown into a pit in the corner of the enclosure. The occupation levels also produced a distinctive collection of fine red vessels imitating samian forms of the late first to early second century, which in all probability were also made in the vicinity.

The early abandonment of the Hardham site might be linked to the development of a considerable settlement on the other side of the river, two miles due east along the line of the supposed Roman road which runs south from Stane Street near Codmore Hill to join with the east-west road leading from Hardham, across the Arun and the Stor towards Hassocks. Evidence of occupation has now been traced over a distance of about a mile along the road.[38] South of the River Stor, between a recurving branch of the river and the marshes of the Arun, is a sandy ridge covered with traces of Roman settlement. One site which has been extensively excavated at Lickfold, near Wiggonholt, is a substantial bath-house (probably part of a larger establishment) which was constructed early in the second century and continued in use well into the fourth century until it succumbed to a devastating fire.[39] Recent work[40] to the south of the building has shown that occupation, including evidence of corn-drying and pottery manufacture, was so extensive that it must be regarded as part of a large settlement rather than just the out-works of a villa estate.

North of the River Stor, again along the line of the supposed Roman road, evidence of occupation is even more impressive.[41] At Holmstreet Farm remains of masonry structures, including a rectangular building with elaborately painted walls, were found stretching for about half a mile. A short distance east of the farm a massive circular structure 40 ft. across internally and with walls 11½ ft. thick was uncovered, constructed in tufa and tiles and with a vaulted roof. Its function must remain unknown but the likelihood is that it served as a mausoleum. Traces of occupation have also turned up in Pulborough village, some three-quarters of a mile to the west, close to the point where Stane Street crossed the Arun. While this remarkable collection of remains could be part of one vast establishment, taken in conjunction with the evidence on the south side of the river, it is better interpreted as a small urban or semi-urban community.

Two other finds deserve mention: a hoard of four lead pigs of late first-century date was found a short distance north of Holmstreet Farm,[42] while in the marshes of the Arun, only 500 yds. north-west of the Lickfold building, a lead cistern decorated with a Chi-rho monogram, proclaiming its Christian connections, was discovered. The context of the cistern is unknown, but its use in the Christian rite of baptism seems to be a reasonable possibility.[43]

It will have become apparent from this brief summary that a remarkable density and variety of occupation exists to the east of Pulborough. Where evidence survives, settlement seems to have begun at the end of the first century, or early in the second, and to have continued well into the fourth century. This may suggest a complementary relationship with the earthwork-enclosed site at Hardham, where the occupation began earlier but had ended by the middle of the second century, by which time the site was being used as a cemetery. It is tempting to interpret this as a shift of occupation from the deliberately established road-station at Hardham to a rather more congenial site along the branch road.

Further along Stane Street, where the road once more crosses the River Arun, is another rectangular earthwork apparently set astride the road. It is only half the size of Hardham, occupying an area of 2½ acres. The lamentable quality of the excavations of 1922-3 prevents adequate description, but the site seems to have begun to be occupied in the Neronian period, as at Hardham, but continued later.[44] It was probably during the late second century that a small building was established within the earthwork, built of timber or half-timber construction with at least one tesselated floor, painted walls, glazed windows and tiled roof. How long the building continued in use it is impossible to say: the coin series, such as it is, ends with four issues of the late third century and a single coin attributable to *c.*350-70, which might be regarded as a stray. The road between Chichester and Silchester was provided with a rectangular enclosure at Iping, comparable to Hardham and Alfoldean, situated close to the point where the road crosses a tributary stream of the River Rother. No excavation has been carried out.

The existence of the three road-stations described above raises the possibility that other major roads may have been provided for in this way. At the point where the Chichester-to-Winchester road crosses the River Meon, at Wickham, traces of Roman occupation of uncertain character have recently come to light, dating back to the Neronian period or even earlier.[45] The scatter of discoveries is such to suggest that the settlement may have been extensive, though no trace of a rectangular earthwork has been found.

A settlement of some significance is also implied by the discoveries made in the vicinity of Hassocks on the junction between the London-Brighton road and the road following the upper greensand shelf.[46] Apart from two Roman villas and a tile clamp all within a mile of the cross-roads, a very substantial cemetery together with extensive traces of occupation was found only 100 yds. from the junction, during the working of a sand-pit. Records are tantalizingly inadequate, but even so it is clear that the cemetery was in use by the Flavian period and continued throughout the second and early third centuries. The coin series shows that occupation, if not burials, extended well into the fourth century. Nothing is known of the settlement itself, but a cemetery or several hundred burials must imply a localized population of some size.

From the above considerations of the minor settlements certain generalizations may be made. At an early date, probably in the Neronian period, road-stations were established at Hardham, Alfoldean, Iping and possibly Wickham. It may be that this was part of a local policy to provide posting-stations (*mansiones*) at regular intervals along the principal routes from Chichester. Hardham is 13 miles from Chichester with Alfoldean 11 miles further on. Iping is also 12 miles from the town and Wickham is about 18 miles. The distances are therefore approximately equivalent to a day's journey.

During the second century, while Alfoldean may have continued as a *mansio*, Hardham (with Pulborough) evidently changed in character and began to take on the aspect of a small nucleated settlement with attendant industry. It was probably at about this time that the settlement at Hassocks grew in size. If the wealth and extent of its cemetery is a reliable indication, it may well have developed as a small urban community to meet the demands for a market centre to serve the richly productive area of east Sussex, which was beyond the economic sphere of Chichester. Both Hassocks and the Pulborough settlement remained in use throughout the fourth century.

Thus it may be said that while the capital, *Noviomagus*, could satisfy the administrative and governmental demands of the cantonal area, it could not wholly meet the economic needs. If it is assumed that the town could serve as a market for a hinterland of up to 20 miles in radius, the vast tract of country east of the river Adur would have been beyond its influence. It was probably for this reason that separate market centres grew up at Hassocks, and possibly at Pulborough.

4.

Rural settlement

The rural settlement pattern of the Regni is characterized by two things: a strong element of continuity, many sites originating well back into the preceding Iron Age or even earlier, and a very marked discrepancy in wealth which appears dramatically within thirty years of the Roman invasion and remains a feature of the social scene until the early decades of the fifth century. The relative distribution of rich and poor settlement is not random. The poorer establishments, the peasant farms and villages, are fairly evenly scattered over the chalk Downs and the coastal plain, but the richer farms — the villas — tend to select various locations where the soil is more productive. They may be said to concentrate in three zones: the Upper greensand ridge at the foot of the Downs, the southern fringes of the Downs, and the coastal plain.

The villas

Perhaps the most surprising aspect of the settlement pattern is the appearance of a group of exceptionally well-appointed villas well before the end of the first century — a phenomenon which distinguishes the Regni from most other tribes of Britain. Five buildings are known belonging to this general category: Fishbourne, Angmering, Southwick, Pulborough and Eastbourne, each of which must be briefly described.

The development of the Fishbourne building is now tolerably well known, as the result of a series of excavations

Fig. 22. A Corinthian capital from the proto-palace at Fishbourne

lasting from 1961 to 1968.[1] Following the phase of military occupation (pp.25-6), a timber-constructed house was put up with what appears to be a detached working area and servants' accomodation immediately adjacent to it. The house itself was a spacious structure of about seven rooms floored with mortar or clay and with walls rendered and painted. The general environment was improved by the provision of drainage gullies, a bridge across a neighbouring stream and by several service roads. The style and quality of the complex would call for little comment were it not for the fact that it belongs to a surprisingly early date in the late Claudian or early Neronian period (*c.* A.D. 50-60). Even more remarkable was its replacement, in the Neronian period, by a substantial masonry building which has been referred to as the 'proto-palace' (fig. 23). This structure, only partially excavated, was made up of several different components. Its range of living rooms was not much more extensive than those of the timber house, but behind them were arranged the luxuries of a colonnaded garden and a substantial bath suite with a large plunge bath and several heated rooms. Beyond this were the servants' quarters.

Not only was the 'proto-palace' well provided with spacious accommodation, it was also extremely elaborately decorated with mosaics, floors composed of coloured stone elements (*opus sectile*) and painted walls enlivened with marble mouldings, while its colonnaded garden was fitted with exotically carved Corinthian columns (fig. 22). The planning and building of this house would have required the importation of large numbers of workmen skilled in arts hitherto unknown in Britain. Furthermore, it implies a patron with Romanized tastes able to foot the not inconsiderable bill. The subsequent development at Fishbourne in the 70s, when a vast palatial building was put up totally overshadowing the 'proto-palace', suggests that the owner may have been the local client king, Cogidubnus. This matter will be returned to later (pp. 79-82).

The similarities between the Fishbourne proto-palace and the villa at Angmering,[2] 14 miles to the east, are striking. Angmering was a substantial establishment of which only the detached bath suite and a series of minor outlying buildings have yet been excavated (fig. 23). The bath suite, approximately the size of the Fishbourne proto-palace baths, consisted of a series of heated rooms built around a cold plunge bath. Like Fishbourne, the decorative finishes included black and white mosaic pavements, *opus sectile* floors and marble wall-inlay. Yet another similarity was that the distinctive tiles used for fitting out the bath-rooms of both buildings must have come

A   Fishbourne (protopalace)

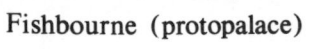

garden

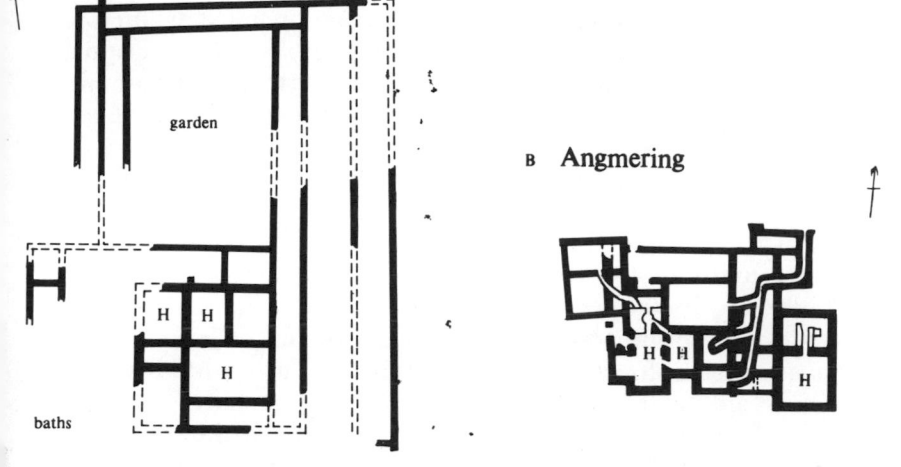

B   Angmering

baths

D   Borough Farm

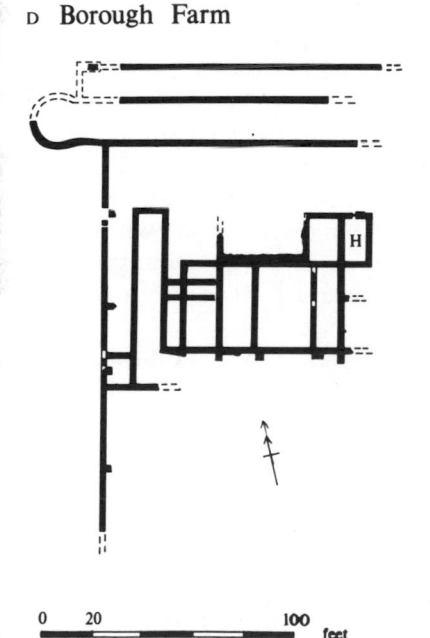

ᴄ   Southwick

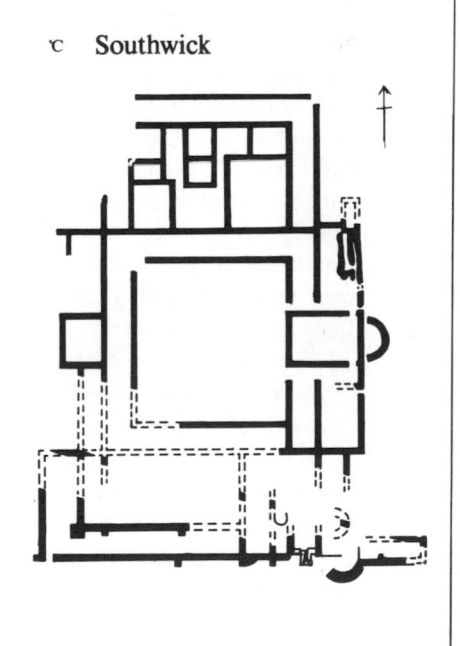

0   20   100
                                feet

Fig. 23. First-century villas at Fishbourne, Angmering, Southwick and
         Pulborough

from the same source. While the dating evidence was sparse, the excavator concluded that construction must lie in the period A.D. 65-75. Thus in date, size, plan and constructional and decorative detail, the two buildings are closely comparable; indeed it is tempting to suggest that they may have been built by the same architect.

Rather less certainty attaches to the date and the affinities of the villa excavated at Southwick in 1931.[3] The plan, though incomplete, shows the building to have been somewhat unusual (fig. 23). It appears to have been laid out and built largely in one operation to create a compact house arranged around four sides of a small square courtyard. The main range of fourteen living rooms lay on the north side of the courtyard, with a bath suite and probably servants' quarters or storage rooms to the south. The centre of the east wing was occupied by a large rectangular structure with a sunken floor, which may have been some kind of ornamental pool. Little is known of the decorative fittings, but quantities of elaborately painted plaster and of loose tesserae imply a high standard while tesserae of glass are suggestive of unusually fine mosaic work. No direct evidence survives as to the construction date, but the pottery and coins recovered were predominantly late-first and second century, which might suggest that occupation had commenced by the Flavian period. Another factor of some relevance is the plan of the north range, with its rooms created by divisions set within a rectangular shell. This style of building is exceptionally rare but compares closely with the north and west ranges of the Flavian palace at Fishbourne.

It is doubtful whether the villa excavated at Pulborough (Borough Farm) in 1907-8 should be included with the early houses (fig. 23),[4] but, as the plan will show, it is of a most unusual layout, incorporating a bath house together with a wide corridor of considerable length terminating in an apsidal recess, and comparing closely in style to the corridor flanking the west wing of the Fishbourne palace. The only indication of a date for the occupation was given by a group of five coins found in the rubbish filling the flue of the hypocaust: four were first-century, with only one of the second century.

The last of the early villas is the ill-known structure built on the cliffs at Eastbourne[5] and now partly eroded into the sea and partly engulfed by modern development. Records, however, show that the site was an extensive one. Its relevance to the present discussion is that it incorporated a quantity of flue tiles of a type known at Fishbourne and Angmering to have been used in Neronian contexts. Thus a first-century construction date seems probable, at least for part of the building.

While it must be admitted that the evidence for first-century villa building among the Regni is uneven, and in some cases uncertain, the fact remains that the Fishbourne proto-palace and the Angmering bath house are indisputably dated to *c.*A.D. 60-75, while a very good case can be made out for including Eastbourne in this group. The claims of Southwick and Pulborough rest largely upon debatable peculiarities of structure and planning, but are supported by the associated coins and pottery. If this can all be accepted, we are forced to conclude that large villa estates were laid out among the Regni in the last half of the first century. Since it is highly unlikely that a tribe which had remained faithful to the Roman cause would have had its rich farmland confiscated and given to immigrant land owners, the villas must reflect the affluence of the local aristocracy left in peace to develop in the strongly philo-Roman atmosphere created by the client kingship of Cogidubnus. How big their individual estates were it is difficult to say until far more is known of the first-century settlement pattern in general, but the spacing of the large early villas may be significant. Each lies on a geographically distinct block of land, Fishbourne west of the Arun, Angmering between the Arun and the Adur, Southwick between the Adur and the Ouse, Eastbourne east of the Ouse and Pulborough isolated north of the Downs. The possibility remains that these vast tracts may indeed represent the territory over which the land-owning aristocracy held control. The hypothesis is attractive, though incapable of proof.

All the early villas continued to be occupied, presumably as the centres of farming estates, but at Fishbourne the house became a vast palatial residence for a brief period of about 25 years before reverting once more to the status of a comfortable villa (fig. 24). The Flavian palace at Fishbourne was constructed some time in the late 70s, making use of the already existing 'proto-palace' which was incorporated as a corner element in the new concept.[6] The central part of the palace consisted of a large formal garden provided with shrub-lined pathways, ornamental trees and fountains, around which four wings were arranged. The west wing contained a centrally placed apsidal-ended audience chamber flanked by state-rooms of decreasing size, while opposite the audience chamber, in the east wing, was sited the main entrance hall which provided access to the entire building. The entrance hall, garden and west wing were all directly accessible to each other and should best be regarded as the official or semi-public part of the concept. Another 'public' room, a vast aisled hall, lay in the north-east corner opening directly on to an external service road. Like similar halls in the palace of Domitian in Rome, it was probably an assembly room of some kind which could be used without people having to go through the palace. The rest of the north wing was arranged to provide suites of mosaic-floored rooms interspersed with quiet, inturned colonnaded courtyards, suitable for visitors. The same arrangment was adopted in the north part of the east wing, the only difference being that here the individual suites were smaller and the gardens were larger, perhaps because they were communally shared by the occupants of the rooms.

The south wing now lies largely beneath the modern main road, but sufficient of it has now been examined to show that it comprised a long range of rooms looking south across a colonnade, continuous along its southern side. In front of the wing, stretching down to the sea, was another vast garden apparently planted with scattered trees and shrubs giving a decidedly less formal appearance than the main garden to the north where everything was laid out with a precise regularity. At its southern limit the garden terrace was revetted by a stone and timber wall, beyond which lay an open sea-water lagoon, dredged so that ships could sail up to the garden edge. There can be very little doubt that this secluded south wing with its private garden and dramatic sea-scape was the preserve of the owner of the palace. The proximity of the

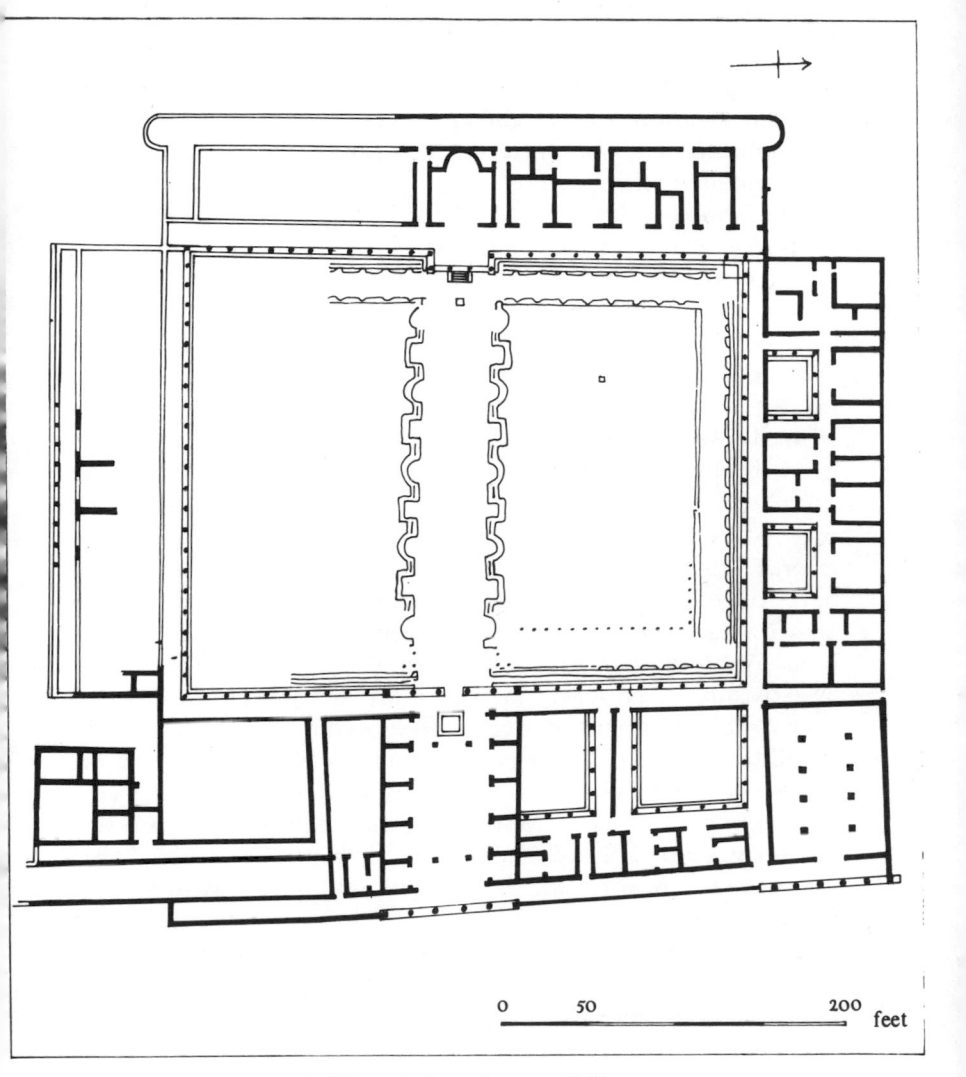

Fig. 24. Plan of the palace at Fishbourne

original suite of baths would have added considerably to his comfort.

The third element necessary to the palace complex, the servants' quarters, workshops and estate yards, are far less well known. North of the building, within a fenced enclosure, traces of milling and baking have come to light, but there was little room for more and it must be assumed that the rest of

the estate lay behind the building to the west. It may even be
that the western arm of the creek was fitted out to serve as a
small harbour at this time, so that produce could be loaded
and unloaded with ease.

The immense size of the palace (more than 15 acres, if the
supposed estate yards are included), the quality of its
architecture and landscaping and the vast area of floors and
walls covered with mosaics (fig. 25), paintings and inlaid marble
leaves no doubt that the building was occupied by a man of
quite exceptional power and wealth. The most likely possibility is that the owner was no less than Cogidubnus
himself. As a client king in the 50s and 60s he would have
lived in some comfort, but not necessarily in great luxury.
The 'proto-palace' would have been quite in keeping for a
man of this status, but after he was raised to the rank of
legatus augusti, probably in the early 70s (p. 26), he would
have needed a far larger establishment, not the least to
provide space for the duties required of an official of this
rank. Another relevant factor is that by the 70s many of the
land-owning aristocracy would have accumulated fortunes
under the Roman system. The wealth of a man like
Cogidubnus, who had been given additional estates by Rome,
must have been considerable. Thus while a reasonable case
can be made out in support of the view that Cogidubnus was
the inspiration behind Fishbourne, it must be stressed that
we have no proof, nor is it likely that proof will ever be
forthcoming.

The phase of villa-building which gripped Sussex in the
first century does not seem to have been repeated with such
intensity elsewhere in the country, although a few early villas
like Eccles in Kent are now coming to light. Far more normal
for Britain was a pattern of gradual development leading
from a native farm built in timber to a simple masonry
building of much the same floor-area, to which sporadically
luxuries such as small baths (fig. 26), underfloor heating and
occasionally simple mosaics with tesselated surrounds were
added. A small number of villas were further elaborated in the
fourth century, but very few reached luxurious proportions.
These generalizations do not, of course, cover all situations: in
some places villas were established on virgin sites late in the

Fig. 25. A first-century mosaic in the palace at Fishbourne
Fig. 26. The bath-house of the Pitlands Farm villa

Roman period, while elsewhere comfortable farms were abandoned long before the fifth century: the more that is learnt of villa development the more it is realized that each example presents its own unique picture. More than 40 villas are recorded in the territory of the Regni. From these a few examples will be chosen to illustrate differences and similarities.

One of the simplest of the Sussex villas is the little house excavated at West Blatchington near Hove[7] (fig. 27). Its site had been occupied since the late Bronze Age and by the beginning of the Roman period a regular farming community had been established, represented now by pits and ditches. Occupation continued in much the same way, the family presumably living in timber houses, throughout the Roman period until, in the third century, a new farmhouse was erected with flint and mortar wall footings, a half-timbered superstructure, mortar floors and a stone-tiled roof. The building itself was quite small, barely 50 ft. wide by 115 ft. long, and was divided into two sections: one was an open-plan aisled hall with its roof supported on four pairs of piers; the other half was partitioned into two rooms and two corridors. The division was a functional one, the hall serving for communal purposes like eating and cooking, while the rooms represent the desire of the owner and his family for privacy and seclusion from everyday domestic activity. Explained at its simplest level, the West Blatchington farm can be seen as an example of continuous occupation spanning 1400 years and culminating in the eventual acquisition of the very minimal attributes of Romanized comfort. Life can have changed little throughout the entire period.

A rather more typical example of villa development is provided by the recently excavated site of Rapsley, Ewhurst[8] (fig. 28), close to the road which branches from Stane Street and runs towards Silchester. The site was occupied from Flavian times, but the first building to be recognized (Period II) was a small four-roomed timber house which appears to have been used throughout much of the second century. The first major phase of rebuilding (Period III) took place about A.D. 200. At this time a large aisled barn was constructed measuring some 40 ft. wide by 100 ft. long,

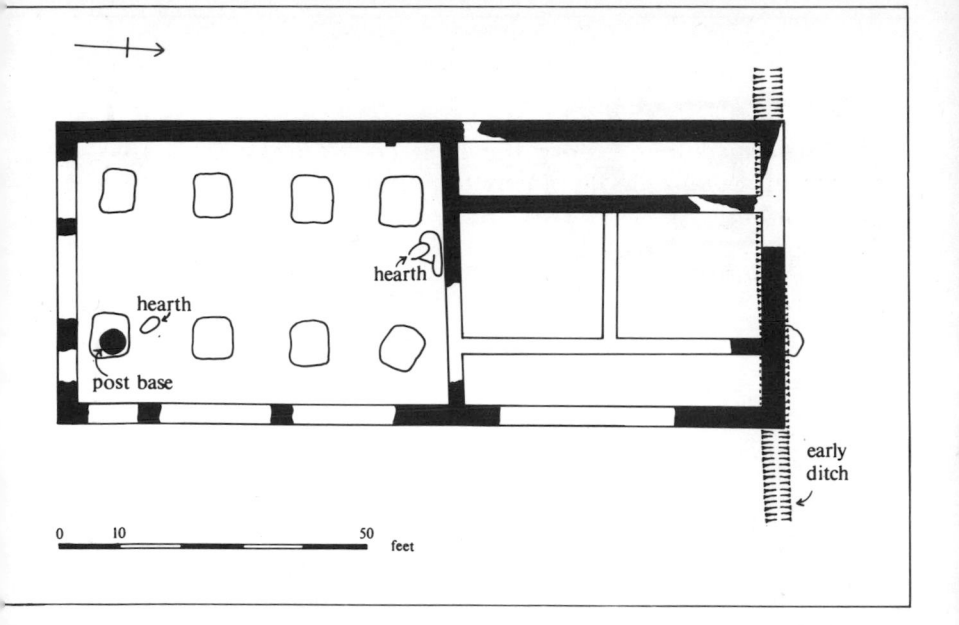

Fig. 27. An aisled farmhouse at West Blatchington

facing a detached bath-house on the other side of an open area. Between the two was a dividing wall which joined with the main southern boundary. It would seem reasonable to suppose that at this stage the main house lay somewhere to the north in the area so far largely unexcavated, unless of course the aisled buildings served as the residential accommodation, which is less likely. After about 20 years drastic modifications took place (Period IV), culminating in the reconstruction of the aisled building and the addition of a new aisled hall laid at right-angles nearby. At the same time the bath block was converted into a small dwelling house, one room of which now possessed a mosaic.

The precise meaning of the Period IV alterations is difficult to understand. Storage space was increased and the establishment seems to have been robbed of its bathing facilities. It can only be supposed that modifications were made to the undiscovered north wing to compensate for the other changes. The final phase of alteration (Period V), which was undertaken in the late third century, consisted of a series of minor adjustments such as the buttressing of the aisled barn and the addition of a room, a back corridor and a front

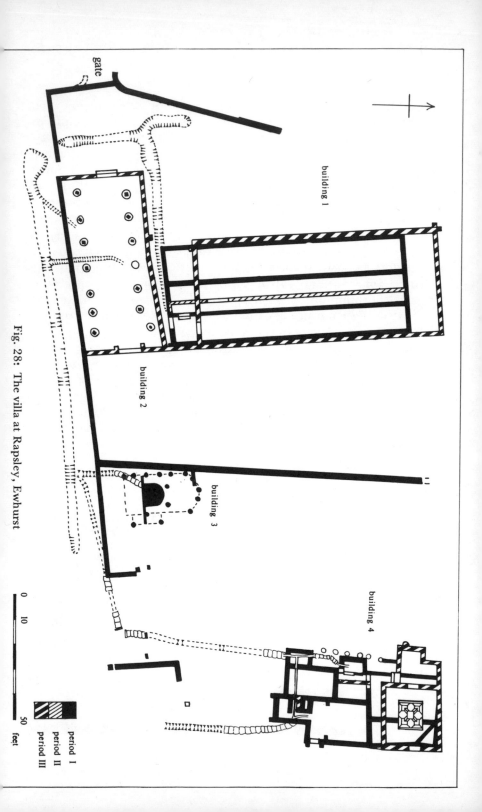

Fig 28: The villa at Rapsley, Ewhurst

gate

building 1

building 2

building 3

building 4

0   10   50   feet

period I
period II
period III

veranda to the dwelling house. Occupation continued into the fourth century but the house was eventually robbed of some of its floor-tiles and finally succumbed to a fire which destroyed much of the superstructure; fire also put an end to the aisled building.

The development of the Rapsley villa demonstrates the growing affluence of the successive owners, but the possibility that one wing remains still to be excavated prevents a final assessment of its significance. From its position within the Weald, corn growing cannot have formed a major part.of the economic support of the estate, although livestock may have been important. Subsidiary works like tile-making and stone-quarrying probably contributed in no small measure and may even have been the principal source of income. It is a reminder that there were other ways to make money in the Roman countryside besides corn.

Two villas which very definitely depended upon corn-production for a significant part of their livelihood lie in the Chilgrove Valley, some 6 miles north of Chichester.[9] The southernmost of the pair (Chilgrove 1) is situated just above the spring line on the lower slopes of Bow Hill, the other (Chilgrove 2) lies close to the Roman road a little below the crest of a neighbouring ridge: both have been extensively excavated under modern conditions.

Occupation of Chilgrove I began in the pre-Roman Iron Age with a cluster of small huts. How the site developed during the first century A.D. is not clear, but early in the second century buildings of timber and flint were in use, culminating in the construction of a simple villa consisting of a single range of rooms fronted by a corridor. During the third century this early villa was rebuilt in more substantial masonry on almost the same plan. Subsequently improvements were carried out, such as the construction of a bath building at the south end of the range (fig. 29), the addition of a polychrome mosaic and an extension at the north end incorporating a heated room with a mosaic floor.

The domestic range looked out across a walled farmyard containing the fragmentary remains of ancillary buildings put up, presumably, for storage, cattle and farm-workers. It was here that the many activities of the farm would have been carried out, ranging from threshing and corn-drying to the maintenance of the farm equipment. Some time after 370 the building was burnt down and thereafter ceased to be used as a high-class dwelling, but more mundane activities of various kinds continued, including the smelting of iron in a large furnace which had been inserted into one of the living-rooms of the main range.

The farm at Chilgrove 2 is a little less well known because excavations are not yet complete. So far no evidence of occupation has been traced before the beginning of the second century but the possibility remains that an early nucleus will be found on the up hill side in an area defined by a massive boundary ditch. The earliest structures on the main site were of timber. This phase was replaced by a very simple masonry-built house comprising only four rooms. Later a large aisled hall was built next to it to serve as a general-purpose shed for various farming activities. It was not until much later, possibly towards the end of the third century, that the first signs of luxury appeared: part of the aisled hall was partitioned off to create three rooms which were added to the accommodation of the residential range. One of the rooms was floored with a tesselated pavement ornamented with circles picked out in a yellow sandstone and variously decorated. The rest of the hall continued to be used for domestic purposes. It was at about this time that a small detached bath suite was constructed, together with a complex of walls bounding the farmyard. Most of the building seems to have been destroyed by fire some time after 360, but the shell continued to be used afterwards.

The contrasts and similarities between the two Chilgrove villas are interesting. Chilgrove 1 was evidently the more important and it could be argued that it served as the residence of the owner-farmer, while at Chilgrove 2 the sparse accommodation and large barn might imply only a resident bailiff, possibly even working for the owner of Chilgrove 1. By the late third or early fourth century both farms had reached a level of comfort suggesting that they were by this time owner-occupied. That they were both destroyed by fire late in the fourth century but continued to be used afterwards is an indication of significant social changes,

Fig. 29. The bath-house at Chilgrove I villa

possibly reflecting the flight of the land-owners to the security of the nearby town of Chichester, from where they could still have administered their estates in safety.

If West Blatchington is the simplest of Roman villas, Bignor provides an example of one of the most complex and elaborate.[10] Situated on the Upper greensand shelf close to Stane Street, it had the advantage both of fertile land and good communications with the market of Chichester, only 10 miles away. Bignor was discovered and extensively excavated early in the nineteenth century by Samuel Lysons, whose general plan is re-drawn here (fig. 30). More recently parts of it had been carefully re-excavated, bringing to light a wealth of detail about the growth of the house before it reached its final grand form. It is not known whether the site began to be occupied in the Iron Age or early Roman period, but by the late second century a small rectangular house built of timber was in existence. It was replaced early in the third century by a simple stone-built villa consisting of no more

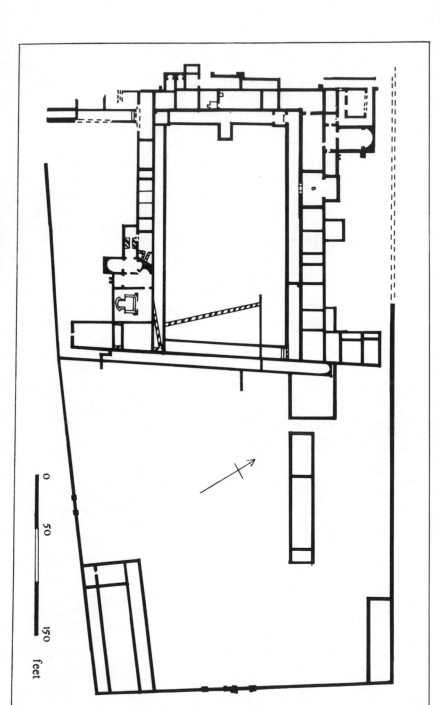

Fig. 30. The plan of Bignor villa in the fourth century

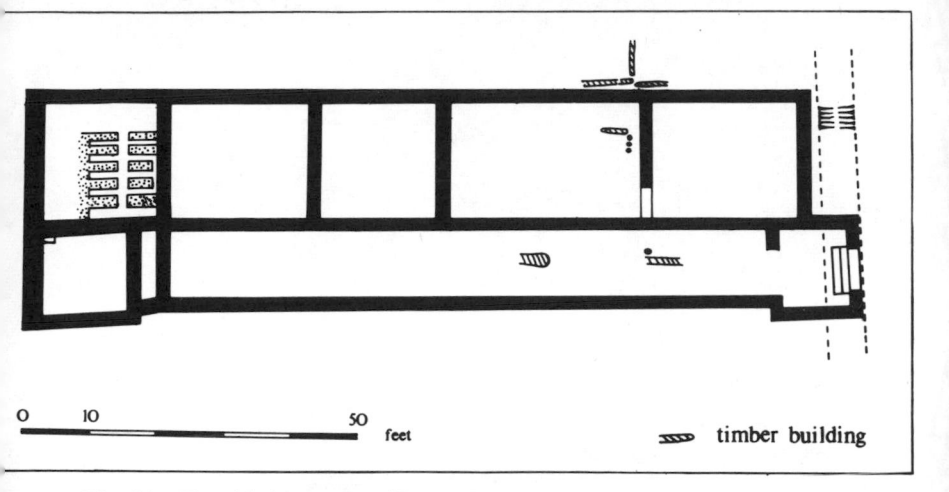

0   10   50
███████████████████████ feet   ⟫⟫⟫ timber building

Fig. 31. The third-century villa at Bignor later incorporated into the
west wing of the enlarged building

than four rooms arranged in a single row. Gradually the
building was improved, first by the addition of a front
corridor or veranda and later by the addition of forward-
projecting rooms at each end, no doubt to increase the
accommodation slightly and to improve the appearance of
the house (fig. 31).

Until this stage, probably towards the end of the third
century, the villa was quite modest and showed little sign of
luxury. Then late in the third or early in the fourth century it
was transformed out of all recognition. The single range of
the original building was incorporated as one side of what
now became a large courtyard house, while at the same time
a small bath suite was added. But this was not the end: later
still a new and far more elaborate suite of baths was built,
including a large cold plunge bath, while a series of additions
were made to the north wing, turning it into what can only
be described as one of the most luxurious suites of rooms in a
Romano-British villa (fig. 32). One of the rooms, evidently
designed for summer use, was floored with a superb
polychrome mosaic depicting a mythological scene in which
Ganymede is carried off by the eagle (fig. 33), the main panel
being surrounded by pictures of dancing girls. As if to
emphasize the summer use of the room, a fountain was
provided towards the centre, its water issuing into a
hexagonal stone-lined basin. The nearby winter room was

Fig. 32. 'Winter' from the Four Seasons mosaic, Bignor

Fig. 33. Ganymede, from a mosaic at Bignor

quite differently constructed with provision for underfloor heating. Its mosaic floor had been magnificent: in an apsidal recess at one end of the room was a panel depicting the head of Venus flanked on each side by birds and simple foliage (fig. 34), while in front was set a border of cupids acting out scenes from gladiatorial training (fig. 35). Unfortunately the centre area of the main floor has been largely destroyed, but there is no reason to suppose that it was any less impressive.

Sufficient will have been said to show that the fourth-century villa with its spacious planning, its many mosaics and its elaborately decorated walls, must have been the home of a very wealthy man. Whether the sudden change in the quality of the building early in the fourth century marked a change of ownership or a rapid economic improvement it is impossible to say, but in either case the owner must have relied heavily on the productive capacity of his estate to provide the surplus wealth needed to indulge his taste for

Fig. 34. The head of Venus, from a mosaic at Bignor

Fig. 35. Cupids as gladiators, from a mosaic at Bignor

comfort and display. Lysons' plan, showing the workshops, stalls and barns built in the outer yard, is a firm reminder that the villa was the centre of a farm, even if the owner might sometimes choose not to be reminded of the fact.

Peasant settlements

The existence of a villa is essentially a reflection either of an imposed politico-economic system, like that implied by the first-century villas discussed above, or of a gradual economic development determined to some extent by the productive. capacity of the land. In both cases it is only to be expected that villas occur where the land is rich enough to support the required level of production, which in practical terms means excluding much of the Weald, with the exception of the very fertile Upper greensand ridge, and the chalk Downs except for the southern valleys floored with rich silts (p. 105). The Weald has always tended to be underpopulated by agricultural communities. Apart from a brief period of active iron production in the sixteenth and seventeenth centuries, it has not supported a large population until recent years when it began to be colonized by London commuters. The Downs, on the other hand, have since Neolithic times been farmed by a gradually expanding population which seems to have reached its peak by the third or fourth century A.D.

One of the characteristics of Downland agricultural settlement is the marked element of continuity which can so frequently be demonstrated spanning the period from the late Bronze Age throughout the Iron Age into the Roman period. Occasionally the settlement occupies almost exactly the same site, but more often there is a slight shift of nucleus within a restricted territory. Movement is, of course, perfectly understandable: a farm occupied for several generations contaminates its immediate environment, making movement periodically necessary.

A classic example of continuous occupation is provided by the site on Park Brow near Cissbury in central Sussex[11] (fig. 36), partially examined according to the standards of the day, in the early 1920s. Although direct continuity cannot be established, three distinct occupation areas have been discovered; a settlement of about eight huts belonging to the late Bronze Age; a settlement of the early and middle pre-Roman Iron Age about 200 ft. away on the other side of a track; and a third settlement, spanning the late pre-Roman Iron Age into the Roman period, some 600 ft. south of the earlier Iron Age occupation. The entire complex is closely interlinked by tracks and fields which must have been in use throughout most of the period represented by the farms. Thus within a distance of some 1300 ft. settled agricultural communities existed for 1400 years.

Of the five houses which constitute the Roman settlement, a description of one will suffice. It consisted of a rectangular platform measuring some 25 ft. by 32 ft., cut back into the downhill face of a lynchet bank of earlier date. The walls were constructed of vertical timbers and infilled with wattle

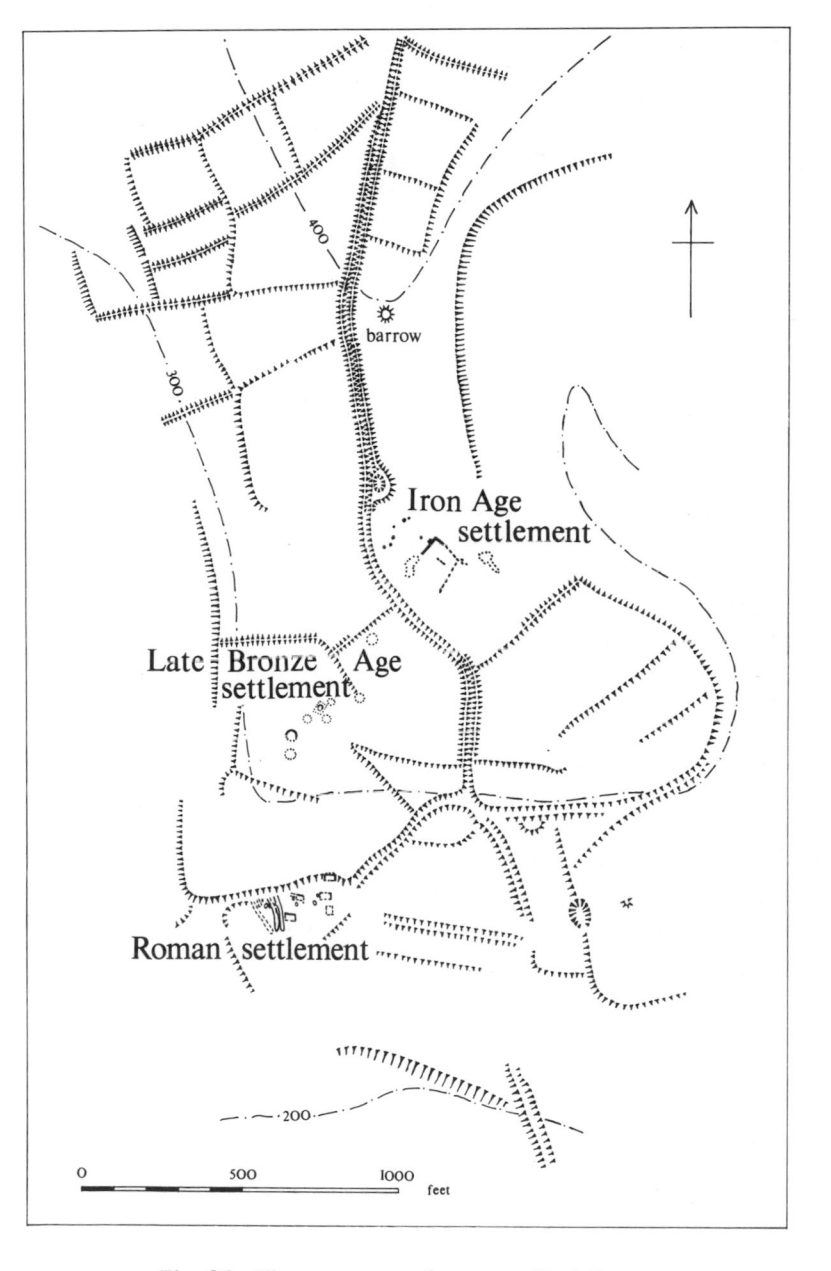

Fig. 36. The peasant settlement at Park Brow

and daub which was keyed internally to take a rendering of plaster painted red. The roof, presumably a simple gable arrangement, was covered in tiles held in position by nails; other traces of the surprisingly sophisticated structure include window-glass and a door-key. It is evident from these structural details that the houses owe much to building methods and styles learnt from urban or villa architecture: together they represent a hamlet of cottages whose occupants, while following traditional practices, were nevertheless able to absorb many new cultural traits from the more advanced society of which they were now a part. Economically they were in direct contact with the Romanized markets, through which they must have obtained commodities such as window-glass, samian pottery, amphorae of wine and shellfish in return, no doubt, for farm produce.

Little can be said of the size of the social unit represented at Park Brow. The eight late Bronze Age huts might be thought to suggest an extended family, but it is impossible to say how many of them were in use at any one time. The five rectangular huts of the Roman period pose the same problems of interpretation but, if all were contemporary, they could represent a unit of between ten and twenty souls.

Many of the elements apparent at Park Brow are characteristic of the hundreds of peasant settlements known among the Regni, but while a number of them have been sampled few have been thoroughly examined under modern archaeological conditions; thus settlement, or even house, plans are few. One settlement at Rookery Hill, Bishopstone,[12] in the east of the area has, however, yielded plans of structures including two ditched enclosures and a rectangular building which would appear to have been constructed on a basis of timber verticals with horizontal sill beams between to take the wattle infilling (fig. 37). The associated pottery suggests occupation within the period from the second to the fourth century.

At Chalton, on the Hampshire-Sussex border, the earthworks of a considerable village of rectangular huts have been planned and are now under investigation.[13] The part of the settlement so far excavated demonstrates a continuity of habitation stretching from the late pre-Roman Iron Age to

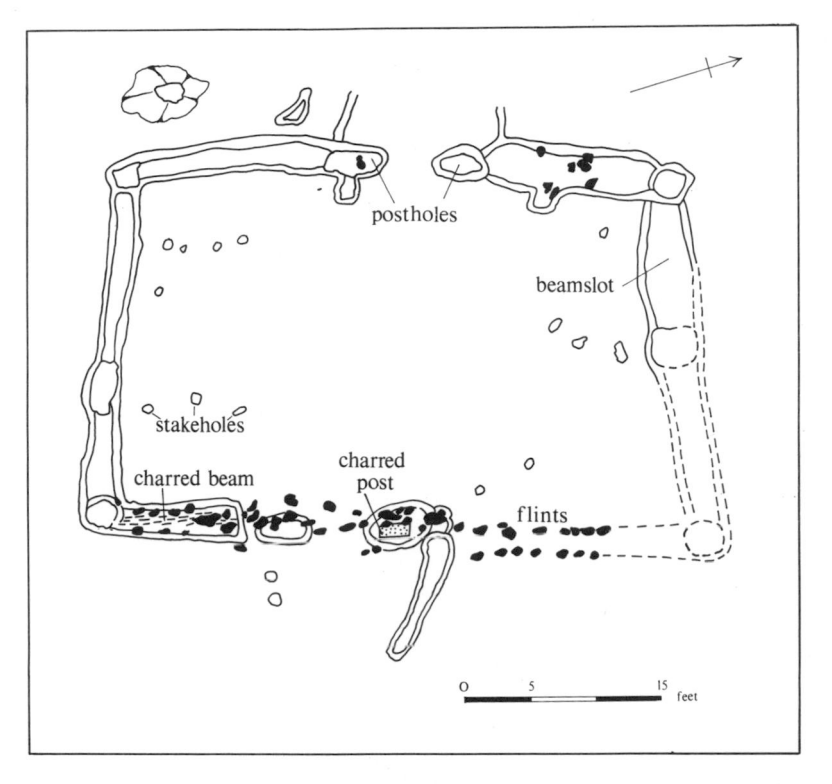

Fig. 37. Timber building from the settlement at Bishopstone

the late third or early fourth century, beginning with a ditched enclosure which was replaced in the second/third century by a number of rectangular houses. Later a small rectangular building of masonry was put up. The earthworks of the settlement are extensive, spreading along the side of a ridge for a distance of 500 yds. While it is possible that this merely represents the gradual shift of a small settlement, the relationships so far demonstrated by the excavation strongly suggest that the Chalton complex is of village size and must be compared to the Romano-British villages identified in Wiltshire. The re-establishment of belief in the existence of villages in Britain is a recent development and comes after a long period when it was thought that all peasant settlements were simple farmsteads.[14] It is now accepted that social

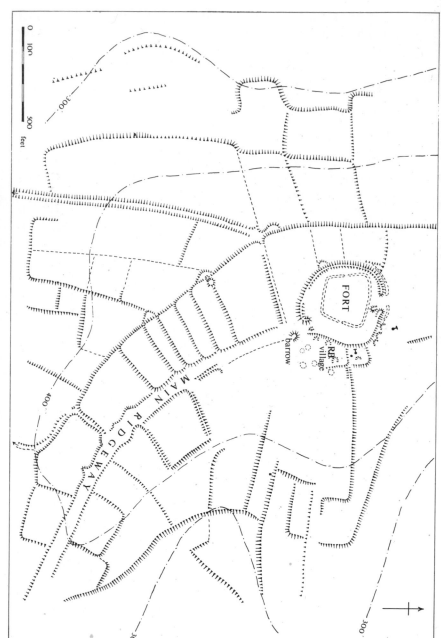

Fig. 38. The peasant settlement at Thundersbarrow Hill

groups varied considerably in size, a variation well represented by the two extremes of Park Brow and Chalton.

Apart from Chalton, relatively few villages are known but this is probably due more to accidents of survival than to an actual lack of sites. One other deserves special mention: on Thundersbarrow Hill,[15] north of the mouth of the River Adur, an extensive settlement was examined by limited excavation in 1932. Its importance lies not in its structural details, for few were recovered, but in its relationship to the contemporary field systems and trackways and to an earlier hill-fort site. The settlement evidently developed alongside the ridgeway, in the late pre-Roman Iron Age. The fields spread right up to the old ramparts, which were partly ploughed away, but respected the ridgeway, leaving it as a swath of unploughed land up to 100 ft. wide (fig. 38). The village remained in use into the fourth century, by which time it was provided with at least one well and a number of corn-drying ovens. While direct evidence of continuity is lacking, it is tempting to see the Romano-British villagers as essentially the descendants of the hill-fort community who first established themselves on the hill perhaps as early as the fifth century B.C. The abandonment of the defences by the middle of the first century B.C. and the shift of settlement to the sheltered eastern slope might have come about in the atmosphere of peace which characterized the political stability of the last few decades before the invasion.

Thundersbarrow is not the only hill-fort site to have been used in the Roman period. A settlement of the first and second centuries grew up just south of the Devil's Dyke near Brighton,[16] while close to Wolstonbury hill-fort a small settlement spanning the second to fourth century is known.[17] Neither, however, need imply a continuity of use from Iron Age to Roman times. The choice of site for Roman re-use may have been quite fortuitous.

A different situation is implied by the two hill-fort sites of Highdown[18] and Cissbury.[19] At Highdown, after a considerable period of abandonment, the defences of the fort were repaired by re-digging the ditch, heightening the rampart and apparently capping it with a timber palisade. Although the excavation within the fort was limited, occupation dating from the late third century associated with a rectangular post-built house has been demonstrated. Superficially, then, it would seem that the long-abandoned fort was re-occupied from the late third century and that at this time or at some subsequent date the old enclosure was put back once more into defensive order. Much the same sequence is implied by the results of the limited excavations at Cissbury, where the area enclosed by the ramparts was subjected to extensive ploughing throughout the Roman period until, during the fourth century or later, the ditch was re-dug and the rampart heightened. Nothing is known of the late Roman settlement within the fort; the situation may not be directly comparable to Highdown but the fact of re-defence implies an occupation of some kind. Perhaps the best context for the re-use of hillforts lies in the social upheavals of the fourth century, but these matters must be left for later discussion (p. 128 ff.).

Farming settlements and the landscape

Some indication has been given here of the variety of rural settlement among the Regni and it is now necessary to examine the relationship of settlement to landscape. Turning first to peasant settlement, the classic statement of Downland occupation was published in 1935 in the form of a map showing the distribution of Celtic field systems and contemporary occupation sites in the Brighton area, that is, on the block of country between the rivers Adur and Ouse.[20] The picture to emerge from this survey was of a densely farmed landscape represented now (or rather, 40 years ago) by discrete blocks of Celtic fields laid out about closely spaced settlements of varying sizes, some of the farms being as little as a mile apart. Villa development was restricted to the dip-slope of the Downs close to the coastal plain where the soil was richer. One important proviso is necessary: what was planned was what had survived. As the original map so vividly demonstrates (though not explicitly) the gaps in the field systems correspond to the presence of medieval villages and their associated fields which would have tended to obliterate all earlier visible monuments, while the spread of the recent urban agglomeration along the coast will have acted selectively against the discovery of peasant settlements at the same time favouring the recording of villas. These reservations apart, the general picture can be accepted.

A rather more detailed study of a much smaller area has been attempted in the region of the medieval village of Chalton (Hants).[21] The results are surprising in spite of the destructive effect of medieval agriculture around the village. What emerges is a highly complex system of land usage involving the preservation of hill-top pasture served by trackways, and the farming of an immense acreage at least comparable in extent to the maximum advance of arable farming in the eighteenth century. Interspersed between the fields and linked by a complex network of tracks are a very large number of settlements of varying size, frequently choosing the crests of the ridges favouring the east-facing slope. Along one crest no less than four sites are known in a distance of a mile, each one originating in a pre-Roman phase of occupation. It is difficult to resist the conclusion that Downland settlement was very much denser than had previously been imagined.

We have suggested above (pp. 95-6) that the gradual development of the Roman villa economy (in contrast to the implantation of villas in the first century) may well be closely linked to the potential of the location, principally the productive capacity of the soil. This is vividly illustrated by the area between the rivers Meon and Lavant (fig. 39). One group of villas, now numbering nine individual buildings, all occupy very similar positions in the valleys dissecting the dip-slope of the Downs. Each lies on the side of its valley somewhere about the 250 ft. contour, which may well have represented the spring-line in the Roman period. Most of the villas are sited at the junction between the chalk uplands and the various sedimentary soils of the valley floors. The advantages of these locations are self-evident: an adequate water supply would be ensured and the range of soils within easy reach of the farm would allow a complex system of mixed farming to be practised. In short, the location was economically favourable.

Where villas have been adequately examined, like the Chilgrove examples, their gradual emergence from simple

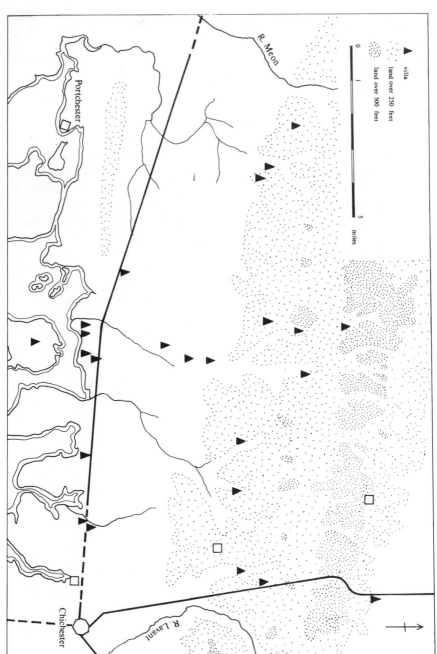

Fig. 39. Villa settlement between the rivers Meon and Lavant

pre-Roman origins can frequently be demonstrated. Although it would be unwise to generalize, it might well be said that those pre-Roman farms in optimum locations were able to be developed into villas while the less favourable sites, like those on the open Downs, remained closer to subsistence level.

A second group of villas are situated along the edge of the coastal strip, served by the Winchester-Chichester road. Very little is known of them except for their tendency to cluster towards the heads of navigable inlets. Benefiting from good communications and a varied environment, their evident wealth may be seen as a direct result of their situation. Much the same applies to the villas along the Upper greensand scarp at the foot of the chalk. The territory of a villa like Bignor would include not only the fertile corn-yielding greensand but also a part of the neighbouring chalk Downs suitable for flocks of sheep, as well as densely wooded claylands within the Weald where swine could find adequate pannage. That villa sites always lie close to a variation in soil emphasizes the importance of mixed farming to the acquisition of wealth within the Roman economic system.

The history of rural settlement

The main lines of the rural history of the Regni must now be pieced together. At the beginning of the Roman period much of the easily inhabitable land seems to have been densely occupied by long-established farming communities. As we have seen, something of the nature and development of this settlement pattern can be traced on the chalk Downs, pointing to the continuous occupation of some sites stretching over 1000 years. Evidence is now beginning to accumulate to show that the coastal plain between Bognor and Worthing was also extensively populated, at least during the Roman period. Since many of these sites appear to have been established on virgin land, it would seem that there was an expansion of rural settlement during the second to third century A.D. Superimposed upon this was the emergence of villa estates, some of them established by the direct investment of large sums of capital, giving rise to the luxury villas of the first century A.D., others created by the gradual ploughing back of profits. By the second century many of the modest farmsteads were beginning to acquire the attributes of Roman luxury, some being rebuilt in masonry for the first time.

How the large early estates fared after the client kingdom had been absorbed into the province it is difficult to say, but all show signs of continued occupation if not of increased opulence. At Fishbourne, which may well be a special case, the old palatial establishment failed to be maintained at its late first-century level of sophistication, but even so the additions and modifications of the second century were far from unimpressive: two bath suites were built in rapid succession and several fine polychrome mosaics were laid at varying times. Even by the mid-third century the standard of living does not seem to have been surpassed elsewhere in the region.

The peasant settlements developed at differing rates, but the adoption of the rectangular house seems, on present evidence, to have been universal by the late second century. Some settlements like Park Brow were able to indulge in luxuries such as glazed windows and painted walls, while at others, like West Blatchington, the owners were able to erect simple but serviceable masonry buildings. It could, of course, equally well be argued that the West Blatchington house was put up by an absentee landlord for his bailiff. The takeover of peasant farms by the large estate owners is a process likely to have become widespread during the Roman period.

Until the end of the third century the process of settlement seems to have been expansive but thereafter certain changes are discernible. The villas at Fishbourne and Preston were both destroyed by fire late in the third century and were not rebuilt, while at West Blatchington and possibly Angmering there is no evidence for occupation after the early years of the fourth century. Southwick, too, may have ceased to have been inhabited by the 340s. The fact that these sites all lie on the coastal plain might suggest that pirate raids were the cause of the abandonments, but there may have been economic factors at work as well.

Inland a number of the peasant settlements were abandoned late in the third or early in the fourth century. Sites like Park Brow,[22] Highdole,[23] Arundel Park,[24] the Devil's Dyke[25] and Charleston Brow[26] all show little sign of fourth-century use. In parallel with this, however, there does appear to have been a marked development at a few large settlements such as Chalton, Thundersbarrow and probably Highdown. It is tempting to interpret this somewhat tenuous data in terms of a process of nucleation, the scatterd farms being abandoned as the population become concentrated in villages. If this hypothesis continues to be supported as more facts are accumulated, some explanation will have to be sought in the economic changes at work in the fourth century. Until then it would be unwise to speculate further.

Many of the villa estates must have outlived the fourth century, a few of them, like Bignor, reaching a spectacular degree of affluence. Others suffered setbacks, like Chilgrove 1 where a disastrous fire destroyed part of the structure after 370, or the nearby villa at Chilgrove 2 where there are traces of widespread destruction after *c*.360. Both sites, however, continued in use for some time afterwards. The latest evidence we have of substantial rebuilding comes from the little known site at Bosham, which is reputed to have a wall dated by the inclusion of a coin of Honorius to after A.D. 395.[27] If the account can be trusted, it is an indication that some villa estates may have lasted as economically viable concerns well into the fifth century.

The rural shrines

One class of site, the rural shrines, managed to escape the vicissitudes of fortune shown by the villas in the later Roman period. Three temples are known: Bow Hill,[28] Chancton-bury[29] and Lancing[30] (fig. 40); all of them belonging to the classic Romano-Celtic type with simple square *cella* surrounded by an ambulatory. All three are sited on hill crests close to the lines of ancient trackways and, more signifi-·cantly, they were all built within 'plateau enclosures' dating back to the early first millenium B.C. (p. 9). It is very tempting indeed to see them as a Roman formalization of religious locations of very considerable antiquity, originally created at, or even before, the period when the 'plateau

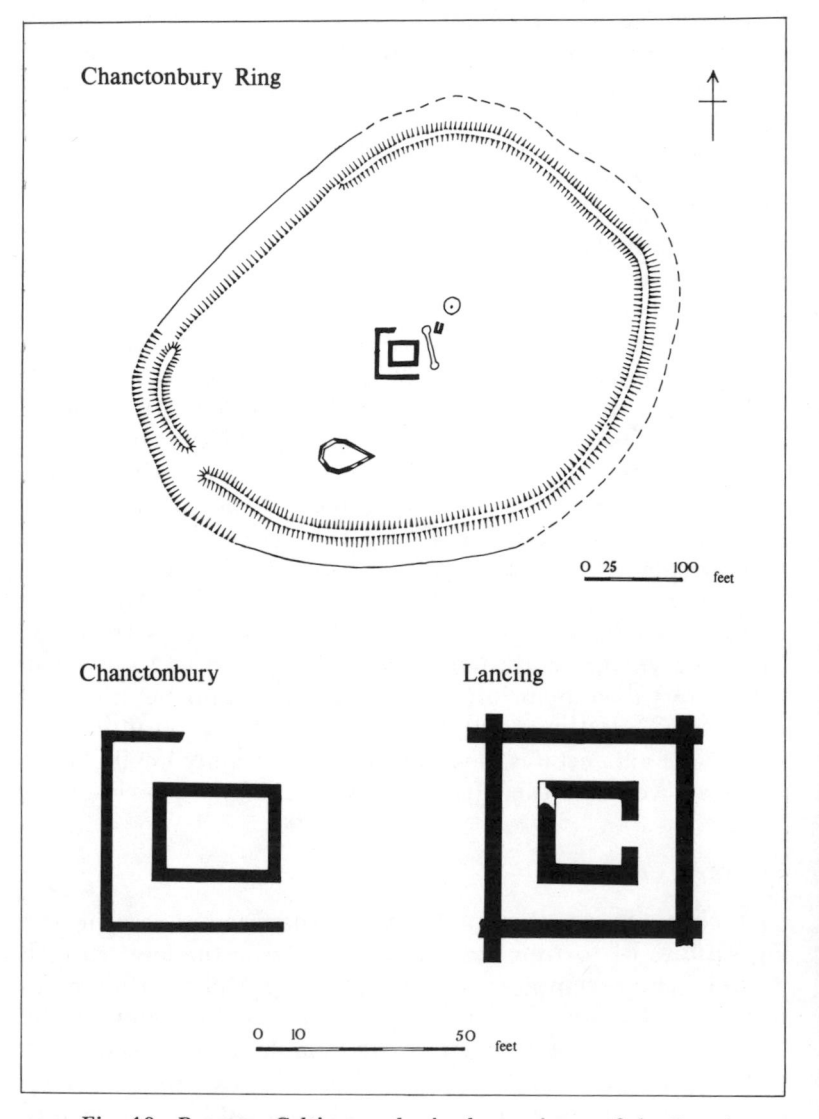

Fig. 40. Romano-Celtic temples in the territory of the Regni

enclosures' were defined.

The temple on Lancing Down clearly post-dated an occupation extending back to the late Bronze Age, to judge by the range of pottery collected from the rather inadequate excavations. All around the temple were small pits containing ashes and sometimes votive offerings, of which the earliest was a simple cremation in an urn of mid-Bronze Age type. The use of the site was, however, densest in the pre-Roman Iron Age when a number of silver coins, possibly a votive hoard, was buried there during the reign of Verica or soon after after.

Chanctonbury is a rather more elaborate complex. The hill top on which it was built was first defined as a plateau enclosure, within which a hill-fort was subsequently built. Later the temple was constructed in the centre of the fort. Nearby were two subsidiary buildings, a strange multi-angular pear-shaped structure some 70 ft. away, and a rectangular masonry cist-like feature opening into a gully which led to a large circular pit. Both were presumably connected in some way with the rituals practised on the site, but their function must remain obscure. The period of use of the site is indicated by a series of coins ranging from a pre-Roman issue through to a coin of Gratian (375-83). The temple on Bow Hill is less well known, but it too was built within an old plateau enclosure and produced an impressive series of coins terminating with Theodosian issues of c.395. Bow Hill is close to the Chilgrove 1 villa which lies on the lower slope of the hill. The discovery there of the base of a statuette of Fortuna made of Caen stone raises the possibility that the figure may have been carted to the villa at some stage from the temple, but it could equally well have been a deity belonging to a household shrine.

The rural temples, then, offer an impressive demonstration of continuity spanning a millenium and a half. They were probably preceded by timber-built shrines originating in the Iron Age which may have continued, suitably repaired on occasions, until the local Romanized community could afford to rebuild them in masonry. Most of them survived the destructive onslaught of Christianity and emerged once more as much-frequented sacred places during the pagan revival of the later fourth century. Thereafter their position is obscure, but they are likely to have remained in use well into the fifth century.

5.

Industry and the economy

Sufficient will have been said in the last chapter to show that farming must have occupied the mass of the population for the greater part of their working lives. It was on the produce of the fields and pastures that the peasants maintained their subsistence level and the villa owners were able to increase their wealth. Corn production remained the corner-stone of the economy throughout the first and second centuries. A survey of Celtic fields in the Brighton region[1] showed that more than 9000 acres were under the plough, i.e. in excess of 18% of the total; bearing in mind the provisos given above (pp. 102-3), the total arable may have been two or three times as great. While it cannot everywhere be proved that all the known fields were farmed during the Roman period, wherever fieldwork has been carried out in detail it can usually be shown that even the outlying fields were being manured in Roman times with occupation rubbish, including pot sherds, carted out from the farmsteads and spread about to help maintain fertility.

It is not yet possible to distinguish with certainty Roman field systems from those laid out in earlier periods. In general terms, however, a difference can be recognized between small square fields haphazardly arranged and systems of long rectangular fields, usually laid out together with a certain order and regularity. The latter may well represent colonization of new land in the Roman period. Classic examples of such an arrangement can be seen at Fore Down, Lullington in Sussex, and at Windmill Hill, Chalton, in Hampshire. At Windmill Hill the fields can, indeed, be shown to have been laid out over at least two settlements of the late pre-Roman Iron Age, totally obliterating them. These examples, typical of large tracts of ancient fields, possibly represent an expansion of settlement with its associated arable during the early part of the Roman period.

There is little direct evidence of the percentages of the various crops grown during the Roman period, but wheat is likely to have been the most favoured: quantities of carbonized wheat grains were found at the village site on Thundersbarrow Hill.[2] Minority crops would have included barley, oats and rye together, presumably, with lesser quantities of leguminous plants. A jar containing some kind of lentil was found in the ruins of the building at Fishbourne, where it had fallen during the final conflagration.[3]

Fields were ploughed with simple ards pulled by pairs of oxen. A small bronze model, found together with other bronzes in a barrow somewhere in Sussex, provides a clear representation of the structure of just such an ard.[4] This particular example is of a type known as a bow-ard, provided with a share shaped like an arrow and with pairs of 'ears', or ground wrests, and a 'keel'. Ards of this type would have been made in wood with only the share covered in iron to prevent wear. The ground wrests were intended to pile up the loosened soil in ridges between the furrows, while the keel gave the whole operation greater stability, allowing the ard to be tilted so as to turn the sod. With such an efficient tool it is unlikely that the pre-Roman method of cross-ploughing, that is the ploughing of a field in two directions at right angles to break the soil, would have been necessary any longer. Herein may lie the reason why the Roman fields were elongaged rather than square like the earlier fields: square fields were the result of cross-ploughing, while long fields were better adapted to single directional ploughing in that they reduced the time spent in turning at the end of each furrow.

One feature found at several of the rural settlements was the provision for drying the grain in specially constructed corn-drying ovens (fig. 41). At Thundersbarrow two ovens were discovered.[5] Each was constructed in a pit 6-7 ft. square and up to 3 ft. deep, in the bottom of which was the flue and stoke-hole built of chalk blocks set in marl. Above the flue was a floor of greensand slabs perforated at the inner end so that the hot air from beneath could enter the upper chamber. It is generally believed that another floor was constructed above this so as to seal in the hot vapours. Upon this uppermost floor the grain would have been laid. The advantage of such an arrangement was that the fire was not in direct contact with the floor supporting the grain, there being an intervening chamber to damp down excessive heating and to prevent the risk of over-parching the seed. No less than eleven corn-drying ovens were found at West Blatchington,[6] ranging in date from the second to the late third century. Provision of this kind must have been quite normal at all farmsteads. The roasting or parching of corn was widely practised in the Roman world: both Pliny and Ovid refer to the process. Among the advantages would have been the prevention of germination during storage as well as the lessening of the risk of rotting and spontaneous combustion.

Tax on wheat production – the *annona* – was substantial. All farmers, whether villa owners or peasants, would have been liable to transport a tithe of their annual yield to the nearest official collecting base, situated in the towns or perhaps at the road stations like Alfoldean, Iping and Hardham. The severity of the tax may eventually have encouraged a general shift from corn production to stock-rearing – a process which is strongly suggested by the evidence from Wiltshire. Unfortunately comparative data is not available from the territory of the Regni.

It is not possible at present to assess in any detail the significance of livestock to the farming economy because no adequate statistics have been published relating to the animal bones recovered during the excavations of farmsteads. In general terms, however, stock-rearing would have formed an essential component of the farming economy. Flocks and herds would be left to browse over stubble fields or on fallow land to provide manure needed to maintain the fertility of the arable, while during the height of the growing season they could be turned loose on the hill-top pastures to fend for themselves. In winter-time cattle would need to be brought in close to the farm for ease of watering and feeding, but sheep could be left out until much later in the season. Pigs would

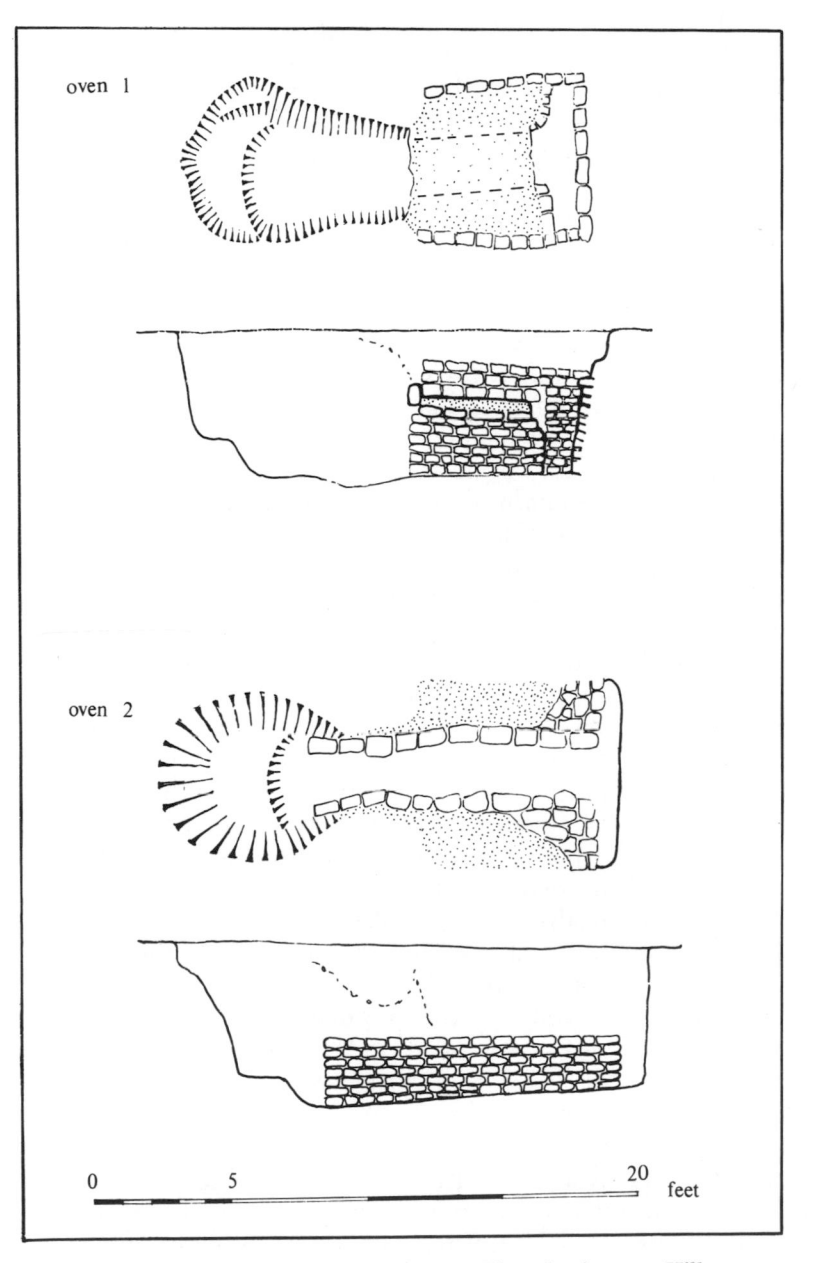

Fig. 41. Two corn-drying ovens at Thundersbarrow Hill

also have played a part in the economy, so long as there was sufficient woodland for them to root in. Where clayland was within easy reach of the farm, adequate pannage would have been readily available, elsewhere the steep hangers or the faces of the lynchets, suitably fenced, would have provided quite sufficient woodland to support substantial herds.

Structural evidence for pastoral activities is not abundant, but many of the Downland pasture areas can be shown to be provided with ditched enclosures for the corralling of livestock, while the depth to which some of the trackways running between fields have worn is indicative of lasting use by cattle. Wherever excavation has been carried out on a reasonable scale on the villa sites, enclosed farmyards have been found as, for example, at Chilgrove 1[7] and at Bignor.[8] At Bignor the yard covers an area of about 90,000 sq.ft. and contains an aisled barn, presumably for corn-storage, and two long buildings which have variously been interpreted as stalls for cattle or pigs. The size of the farming installations here must reflect the extent of the estate. At Chilgrove, an altogether more modest establishment, the yard occupies only 10,000 sq.ft.

Viewed as a production centre, a farm would yield a marketable excess of corn, hides, wool, sinew, lard, meat, timber and possibly fruit, honey and milk. In exchange for these it would acquire money for wages and for hoarding and subsequent investment, a wide variety of foodstuffs such as salt, shellfish, wine and oil, and consumer goods ranging from trinkets like brooches and bracelets, tableware of pottery, pewter or even silver, to more substantial purchases including perhaps statuary. Thus the expansion of the farming economy not only satisfied the fiscal needs of the province and provided food for the population, it also stimulated other kinds of production and trade.

Pottery manufacture

No one excavating a Roman site can doubt that the average community expended vast quantities of pottery. It is hardly surprising, therefore, that local production centres should emerge in response to the demand. The territory of the Regni was provided with two principal sources of potter's clay: the Gault clay which runs in a band of varying width along the edge of the Upper greensand shelf, and the Reading Beds — a sticky red-and-grey mottled clay outcropping sporadically along the edge of the dip-slope of the chalk. Both sources were utilized throughout the Roman period. One of the earliest potteries to be recorded is that already mentioned in describing Chichester. Here two well-built kilns produced a series of fine wares, including Gallo-Belgic style butt beakers, for the local market of the 50s and 60s.[9] Although the Chilchester kilns were not directly sited on their clay source, Reading Beds clay would have been available close by. The emergence of specialized kilns at this early date is a direct result of the process of supply developing to serve the demand. By the late first century several local production centres were at work including one which was manufacturing specialized lead-glazed wares in rather inferior fabrics.

Another late-first-century workshop grew up somewhere in the Hardham-Pulborough area, making fine red ware imitating imported samian vessels.[10] Its products were transported along Stane Street, north to Alfoldean and south to Chichester and Angmering. These Hardham potteries must have been using the Gault clay which outcrops nearby. While the imitation samian vessels ceased to be made early in the second century, a vigorous pottery production centre was maintained in the area throughout the second and third centuries.

A large centre also developed in the Rowlands Castle valley, north of Havant, utilizing the Reading Beds clay.[11] Kilns and waster heaps extend over a considerable area, reflecting an industry which appears to have originated at the end of the first century and to have continued in production into the end of the third century. The out-put was entirely geared to the coarseware market, concentrating on the production of bowls, jars and lids made in a plain grey ware. It would seem that the potters developed a monopoly, their wares appearing to the virtual exclusion of all others over a territory stretching from the River Meon to Chichester. The short length of road which leads south from the kilns to the

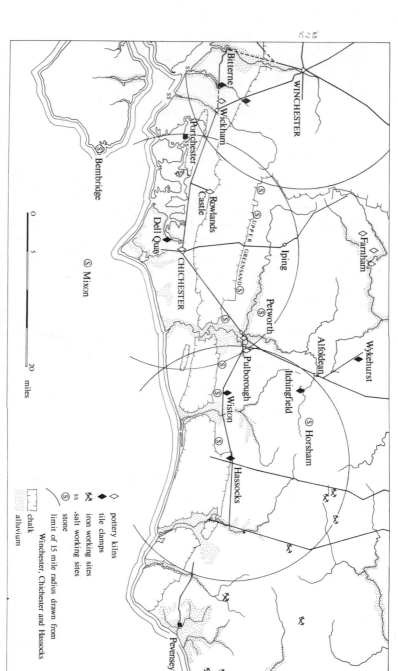

Fig. 42. Industrial sites and natural resources in the territory of the Regni

WINCHESTER
Bitterne
Wickham
Porchester
Rowlands
Castle
Dell Quay
CHICHESTER
Bembridge
Mixon
UPPER GREENSAND
Iping
Farnham
Petworth
Alfoldean
Wykehurst
Pulborough
Itchingfield
Wiston
Horsham
Hassocks
Pevensey

0 5 20 miles

◇ pottery kilns
◆ tile clamps
✗ iron working sites
ss salt working sites
Ⓢ stone
   limit of 15 mile radius drawn from
   Winchester, Chichester and Hassocks
   chalk
   alluvium

main coastal road may well have been constructed specifically to serve the centre.

If the Rowlands Castle kilns satisfied the coarseware needs of the area between the Meon and the Lavant, and the Pulborough-Hardham kilns served the territory from the Lavant to about the Adur, it seems reasonable to suppose that another coarseware production centre lay somewhere in east Sussex to accomodate the area east of the Adur. That the pottery from the area shows certain typological similarities tends to support the idea, but so far no trace of the kilns has been found. They might, however, be expected to turn up somewhere along the Gault clay band, possibly in the region of Hassocks.

In addition to the marketing of local pottery for general domestic use, there was a widespread trade in finer wares. Vast quantities of samian pottery were imported into Britain and distributed, presumably via London and Chichester, to all parts of the region — even the remotest peasant settlement was able to acquire a few vessels. The samian kilns usually produced plates and bowls for export; to complete the table service, beakers from the Nene Valley potteries and from the Rhineland were imported. These, too, were widely distributed to all social levels.

By the late third or early fourth century there seems to have been a significant change in the production and distribution of pottery. The market was now dominated by a few very large concerns, most of them outside the area. Black-burnished coarseware was produced in quantities in the Poole Harbour area and presumably shipped along the coast for off-loading to the local markets, while a rather wider variety of coarsewares made in the Farnham area were transported by way of Stane Street to Chichester for secondary distribution. The place of the imported tablewares was taken, in the west of the region, by the produce of two big kiln groups, one in the New Forest and the other in the Oxford region, both manufacturing a range of colour-coated bowls, beakers and mortaria and both competing for a share of the consumer market. Somewhere in east Sussex another pottery was turning out much the same range,[12] evidently capturing the bulk of the market east of the Arun, its products also occurring in small quantities at Chichester, while a few vessels even found their way to Portchester. The location of this centre has still to be found, but it is most likely to be somewhere along the Gault clay band east of Pulborough.

The situation changed little throughout the fourth century, the five large centres continuing to produce most of the pottery in everyday use. In parallel, however, there developed two curious groups of pottery, both of them hand-made. One class, found in some quantity at Portchester from the late third century onwards, evidently copied regular wheel-turned jars, dishes and plates and was in use together with them.[13] The other class, known as Thundersbarrow ware,[14] consisted of very large hand-made storage jars which have been found on many of the fourth-century sites in Sussex, spreading as far west as Portchester. The exact meaning of this hand-made pottery is difficult to understand unless it represents the attempts of unskilled locals to capture a part of the market. The relatively high percentage of hand-made wares at Portchester speaks of some measure of success, at least locally. The wider distribution of the Thundersbarrow jars is more puzzling but a possible explanation is that they may have been specialized containers used to transport a single commodity such as salt or honey.

Tile kilns

One of the dramatic changes brought about by the imposition of Roman rule was the rapid development of the extractive industries concerned with the production of building materials. To begin with, the demand would have been largely for timber and tiles. Enormous quantities of timber were required for laying out the early town of Chichester and the constant demand for tiles throughout the Roman period must have continued unabated, particularly as even peasant settlements used tiles as a roofing material. Five tile kilns are at present known within the area (fig. 43). One was situated on the Reading Beds clay at Dell Quay near Chichester; another lay on the Gault clay a short distance from Hassocks; while the other three, Itchingfield, near

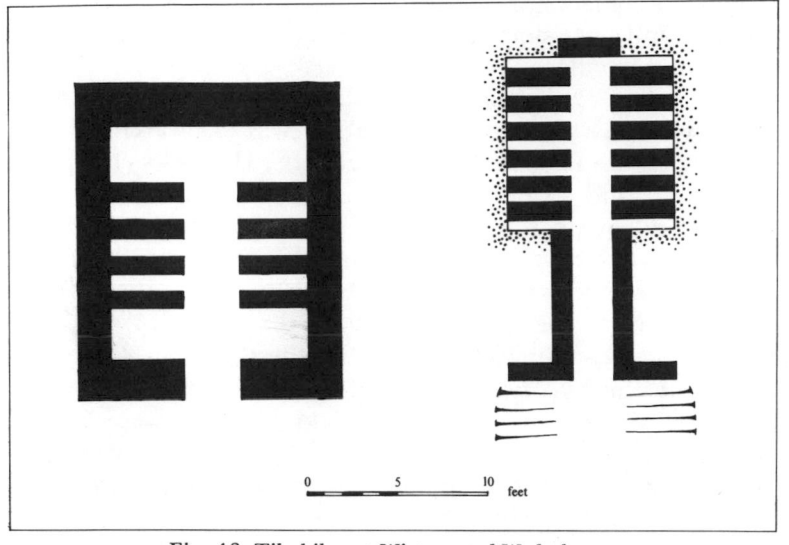

Fig. 43. Tile kilns at Wiston and Wykehurst

Alfoldean, Wykehurst, near Cranleigh, and Wiston, some six miles from Pulborough, all made use of the thick Wealden clays.

The clamp at Wykehurst on the estate of the Rapsley villa (pp. 84-7) is the best known.[15] It consisted of a kiln chamber just over 9 ft. square divided by six parallel supporting walls, through the centres of which ran a series of arched openings continuous with the main arched flue. The flue opened into a large stoke-hole. The functioning of the clamp was simple: the tiles, after a sufficient period of drying in the adjacent yard, would have been stacked up on and over the supporting walls, leaving sufficient space between them for the circulation of the hot gasses. When the clamp was built, the whole structure was enclosed with clay bricks, and firing began. After a set period under reducing conditions, stoking stopped and the clay covering bricks were pulled away to allow the tiles to cool slowly, the presence of oxygen creating the characteristic red colour of the surface layers. When the cooling process was complete, the tiles would be removed and the clamp cleared of wasters and ash ready for the next batch. The Wykehurst clamp produced a range of tiles including tegulae, imbrices, combed box-tiles, building bricks, tesserae and pear-shaped roof tiles, all designed for use in the neighbouring villas.

The other clamps are less well known. Wiston is of the same type at Wykehurst, but the site was excavated in 1848 and details are obscure.[16] Similarly, the Hassocks clamp was discovered and examined in the nineteenth century and is without adequate record. The Itchingfield clamp, which has been partly excavated,[17] produced voussoir box-tiles, tegulae, imbrices, pilae tiles and bricks, while the unexcavated clamp at Dell Quay has yielded a quantity of debris suggesting the same wide range of products.

The proximity of three clamps to nucleated settlements is probably significant. The Itchingfield products were used in quantity at Alfoldean, while the Dell Quay tiles turned up at the second-century bath building at Fishbourne as well as in Chichester. Presumably the Hassocks clamp also served the needs of its immediate neighbourhood. There were, no doubt, many more clamps in existence, each one springing up as a local need arose, only to be abandoned when it had been satisfied.

Somewhere in the region at least two specialized tile works had been in production but the exact location of neither is known. One provided a highly distinctive range of tiles including complex box-tiles for the Neronian and early Flavian phases of the buildings at Fishbourne[18] and Angmering,[19] some of its wares being transported for use in the presumably contemporary building at Eastbourne.[20] It can only be supposed that the clamp was short-lived and that it was worked by an experienced tiler employed for the specific purpose of manufacturing the fittings for these constructions. The other centre produced a distinctive type of box-tile ornamented on the surface with designs impressed by roller stamps. These tiles, which were fairly widely spread over south-east Britain in the second century,[21] occurring for example in one of the late Fishbourne bath buildings, may well have been produced somewhere in the Weald within the territory under discussion. The quality of the work and the distribution of the products suggests that the workshop was of some importance.

The stone quarries

Tile making was only one aspect of the construction industry. The exploitation of building stone must have employed a significant percentage of the population, particularly after the late second century, by which time the fashion for masonry building had become established. For the most part, buildings were of flint and mortar. In chalkland areas flints could be gathered from the fields and the mortar could easily be manufactured by burning chalk to form lime and mixing it with suitable aggregate acquired from the copious gravel beds of the coastal plain around Chichester. The exploitation of these materials would have involved little specialist knowledge or organization and could well have been carried out by estate labourers in slack periods between the farming routine. The extraction of other types of building stone was, however, a more involved process. Basically the territory could provide four sources: Upper greensand, Mixon limestone, Horsham sandstone and ferruginous sandstone from the Lower greensand beds. The Upper greensand was one of the most popular by virtue of its ease of cutting and its relative durability. The superstructure of the Fishbourne palace was entirely built in greensand and the external face of the Chichester city wall was clad with it. Elsewhere it was sometimes used for quoins in flint-built structures. The Mixon limestone, a much harder rock collected on the shore from the Mixon reef now some distance off Selsey Bill, was rather more restricted in its use but is known at Fishbourne and Chichester. Yet, in spite of its durability, it does not seem to have been transported far afield. The remaining two types of stone both come from the central Weald and both had rather limited use. The principal characteristic of the Horsham stone, the way in which it laminates, gave it a specialized significance as a roofing material in place of tile. The Chilgrove villas, for example, were partly roofed with it.

Relatively little building stone was imported into the area except from the Isle of Wight, which produced Bembridge limestone used in quantity at Fishbourne in the first century

A.D. Again, in the late third century, limestone together with various types of sandstone was imported from the Island for certain detailed construction work at Portchester. The proximity of both Portchester and Fishbourne to the sea would have made it cheaper and quicker to transport boatloads of stone from the Island rather than to convey it by road from further inland. Stone for more specialized uses, such as the columns of the Flavian palace at Fishbourne, was brought in from even further afield, from the West Country and from Northern France, but this seems to have been an exceptional occurrence and should not be allowed to overshadow the fact that most of the building stone needed in the region was produced locally.

Decorative stone for inlays, mouldings and inscriptions was largely restricted to Purbeck marble imported from Dorset, presumably by sea.[22] The Cogidubnus stone and the Nero dedicatory inscription were both carved on slabs of Purbeck marble and large quantities of the stone were used at Fishbourne and Angmering for decorative purposes. Sussex produces a somewhat similar material known at Petworth marble, which can be easily confused with the Dorset variety. Examples of the Petworth stone have been found in Roman contexts and it may be that its use was more widespread than is at present realized. It is possible that some of the so-called Purbeck marble may turn out, on more detailed examination, to have come from the Petworth beds. The Weald also produces a dark-grey mudstone which was used for decorative inlay at Fishbourne and at Bignor, where slabs of it, alternating with slabs of hard chalk, floored a large room in the bath suite, giving it a chequer-board appearance. Exotic marbles were imported, but only in limited quantities. At least one boat-load must have been brought in during the Flavian period to provide the range of foreign marbles used for veneering in the Fishbourne palace, but other than this the decorative stone employed in the region was locally produced in the south of Britain.

The iron industry

One of the principal exports of the Regni, beside farm

produce, was iron.[23] The rich ferruginous rocks of the Hastings and Ashdown sands were extensively worked, particularly during the second and third centuries, continuing traditions already well established in the pre-Roman Iron Age. Although most of the better-known sites lie beyond the limit of our territory, some passing reference must be made to them for the light that they throw on the industry in general.

During the Roman period production was on a very large scale. At Beauport Park, near Hastings, quantities of slag and cinder have been found covering 2 acres, suggesting continuous and concentrated working over a long period; while at Oldlands, near Maresfield, it is estimated that beds of iron slag from 2 to 10 ft. deep extend over an area of 7 acres. Where the Roman road from London to Lewes was laid out past the workings, iron slag was used to metal it for a stretch of several miles.

The only site to be examined in any detail, Bardown near Wadhurst, on the south bank of the River Limden, has proved to be a considerable industrial complex incorporating ore-roasting and iron-smelting furnaces, slag heaps and a settlement for the workers.[24] It would appear that the settlement site was founded *c.*A.D. 140-50 and iron continued to be extracted there for 50 years. Early in the third century production ceased at the main site and was transferred to satellite sites while the original nuclear settlement continued in use, probably until the end of the third century. The sequence is interesting, for it underlines one of the principal difficulties of iron extraction — large quantities of wood were required. After a relatively short period of production, the neighbouring forest would have been used up and it would have become more economical in terms of labour to set up new smelting works where the forest cover remained, while at the same time retaining the settlement installations at the original base.

The organization of the Wealden iron industry is largely unknown, but in theory all mineral rights were vested in the State. It is therefore a distinct possibility that the mines and extraction plant were State-owned. Some support for this view comes from the iron works at Bardown, Beauport Park,

Cranbrook and Crowhurst Park, where tiles stamped with the letters CLBR (*classis Britannica*) have been discovered.[25] This association with the British Fleet could suggest that the navy stationed on the Kentish coast was in some way responsible for organizing and maintaining the iron output on behalf of the government. The theory is attractive but difficult to prove.

All of the iron works so far known lie to the east of the Brighton to London road in an area of the Weald well served by three principal north-to-south roads and a mass of minor trackways. Whatever· the organization of the industry, there can be little doubt that the enormous quantity of iron produced (an estimated 10,000 tons for Bardown alone) was transported by road to London and probably by sea from a port situated somewhere near Hastings. If, as seems reasonable, the industry was controlled by the navy, part at least of the output may have found its way north to the military zone.

The organization of the iron industry on a large scale does not, on present evidence, seem to have come about until the second century. Before that, iron was being extracted in the Weald in smaller quantities, usually at sites which originated in the pre-Roman period. Iron ore was also transported to Chichester for local working. At an excavation in North Street[26] late first-century levels were found to contain slag, furnace lining and hammer scales, implying both extraction and the working of the bloom into a relatively slag-free wrought iron. Another late-first-century smithy was found on the Westgate site.[27] While it must be admitted that the evidence is at present meagre, it is not impossible that a 'free trade' in iron working existed all the time that the client kingdom was maintained and that the State takeover did not occur until after the death of Cogidubnus.

Salt manufacture

One product, which remained of very great importance to the economy, was salt. Salt workings originating in the Iron Age lined the creeks between Portsmouth and Chichester harbours, and there can be little doubt that the river estuaries further east supported extensive salt-producing industries. The extraction process was fairly complex, involving both natural evaporation of sea-water and the boiling of the salt-rich liquor. The salt crystals would then have been packed into containers for transport and marketing. Any territory, like that of the Regni, blessed with a long sea-frontage, would undoubtedly have developed its salt-producing industry as an integral part of the tribal economy. Whether the production was handled by the local estate owners or by specialist firms is, however, unknown.

Finally, the sea itself should not be overlooked as a source of income. The estuaries must have been as extensively cropped for their shell-fish as the land was for its corn. Oysters, mussels and cockles were consumed in enormous quantities all over the country. Shop-keepers in inland towns like Winchester and Silchester may well have had regular contracts with suppliers in the coastal regions, providing yet another source of wealth for the area.

Sufficient will have been said to show that the territory of the Regni was rich in natural resources. It could provide corn, meat, shell-fish and salt in excess for export, it could satisfy most of its own needs for pottery and building materials, and it may well have derived some benefit from its iron resources, even though these may have been worked for the State. In short, the territory was largely self-contained and its more influential inhabitants can have had little difficulty in maintaining high standards of living.

6.

The late fourth and fifth centuries

The year 367 was a turning point in the history of the country, for in that year, following earlier rumblings, the Picts, Scots and Attacotti, possibly aided by the Saxons and Franks, descended on the Roman province in force.[1] The great 'barbarian conspiracy', as it was called by the historian Ammianus, was both violent and successful: Hadrian's Wall was completely overrun though fully garrisoned at the time, the Count of the Saxon Shore (*comes maritimi tractus*) was killed and the military leader of Britain (*dux Britanniarum*) was taken prisoner. The province, we are told, was in chaos south to the Thames: civic order had broken down, large numbers of escaped slaves and military deserters joined in and the countryside was infested by bands of looters bent on plunder. It was to remain so for a year, until eventually Count Theodosius, leading four regiments of the field army, landed in peace at Richborough and marched on London to begin the task of re-establishing order. By small scale military operations rounding up dissidents and by offering a general amnesty to deserters, he was gradually able to bring the province back under control. Having pacified the south and reconstituted the civilian and military administration, he cleared the rest of Britain of rebels and invaders and finally set about reorganizing the frontiers.

The events of these two vital years must have left their mark on the territory of the Regni, not the least because of the need to up-date the defences of its extensive sea-board. Whether or not the civil unrest spread this far south is less certain, but there are some hints among the villas of the area that all was not well. Both of the farms near Chilgrove, only a few miles from Chichester, show signs of rapid decline after fires in the 360s and 370s, and remarkably few villa sites in Sussex have yielded coins dating to after 370, although it can hardly be doubted that the great estates like Bignor survived the unrest. Before any meaningful generalizations can be made, however, more excavations conducted to modern standards are required.

The history of the two shore forts of Portchester and Pevensey is now tolerably clear. As the coin sequence shows, Pevensey was maintained as a strong-point well into the early years of the fifth century and possibly even later[2] (p. 137). It may have been at this time that the outer ditch was re-dug defending the land approach to the west gate, while the discovery of two tiles stamped HON AUG ANDRIA, referring to the emperor Honorius, must represent building work presumably carried out by the military leader Stilicho, who commanded Britain on the emperor's behalf in the closing years of the fourth century. Pevensey, therefore, was retained as a fortress after the reorganization of 369.

The fate of Portchester appears to have differed.[3] The coin sequence shows a marked decline in numbers after 367, although a few later issues are known extending into the fifth century. The contrast with Pevensey (and other shore forts like Richborough) is so marked that it must be supposed that the garrison had been removed from Portchester by about 370. The Solent could not, however, be left undefended since it commanded the approach to the rich hinterland of Wessex – an obvious target for pirate attack. In fact the garrison seems to have been moved only a short distance to Clausentum (modern Bitterne) on Southampton Water, where a substantial fort was built, its walls dated by the inclusion of a coin of 367.[4] The reason for the shift is obvious enough: for the fleet to reach the Solent from Portchester would have meant negotiating the narrow channel at the mouth of Portsmouth Harbour which, under certain conditions of wind and tide, was treacherous. Clausentum provided a far more suitable base with adequate protected anchorage, good land communications and an untroubled approach to the Solent. The shift from Portchester to Clausentum can be seen as an example of the care with which Count Theodosius reorganized the defences of the Province.

The evacuation of Portchester by its garrison did not mean the end of occupation, far from it. The mass of late domestic debris which was allowed to pile up inside the walls, spreading out over some of the roads, is evidence that people continued to inhabit the fort. The nature of this occupation is obscure, but it may be that a small holding force of military personnel was stationed within the walls, perhaps together with a substantial civilian population. The later history of the site in the fifth century (p. 138) would support the idea of a continued military presence which in any event would have been a sound defensive measure.

At Chichester the addition of bastions to the city wall and the recutting of the ditch in a wide flat-bottomed form may reasonably be assigned to the Theodosian reorganization, although positive evidence of dating has not yet been obtained (pp. 67-8). The discovery of a late Germanic type of belt buckle at the County Hall site is an indication that Chichester, along with many other towns in Britain, may at this time have been provided with a small defensive militia (p. 68).

If Clausentum and Pevensey were the key-points in the Theodosian system with smaller garrisons at Portchester and Chichester, the immediate question to arise is: how was the coast between Chichester and Pevensey — a distance of some 50 miles — protected, for protection of some kind was surely needed? One answer would be to suppose that other fort sites once existed but were subsequently destroyed by coastal erosion, but there is another possible explanation: could not some or all of the three refortified hill-forts, Highdown,[5] Cissbury[6] and the Caburn,[7] have served as strong-points in the late-fourth-century system? The policy of re-using old earthworks is well known along the German *limes* at this time and need occasion no surprise.[8] Whatever may be thought of the claims of Cissbury and Caburn, Highdown is a more attractive possibility, both in its proximity to the sea and in the density of fourth-century occupation within. Its later use as a cemetery in the fifth century could imply continued occupation. Further excavation of this vitally important site is badly needed before the problem can be pursued further. During the first flourish of the Theodosian restoration Britain managed to maintain a standard of civilized existence, but between 383 and 407 the stability of the province was continually weakened by the gradual withdrawal of troops to fight on the continent, in theory to protect Britain but in reality to support the personal aspirations of their commanders. In 383 under Maximus, 401 under Stilicho and 407 under Constantine III, armies amassed in Britain were shipped to the continent to fight and be beaten: very few would have returned. This drastic depletion of the available manpower must be seen against social trends in general. The empire, and presumably Britain too, was faced with a constant and worrying decline in the birth-rate. So serious was the situation that edicts were passed preventing people from giving up their inherited professions in an attempt to stop the increase in the mobility of labour. But gradually the situation worsened: land was abandoned and the dislocated peasantry either gravitated to the security of the large estates to become *coloni*, or opted out altogether to join the ranks of the robbers (*bagaudae*) who were becoming a serious threat to law and order in many parts of the Roman world. Thus there were three principal effects: the growth of large, almost feudal estates; the abandonment of the smaller farms and land; and the concentration of cities on their own defences. Some would argue that there was also a growing alienation between the peasants and the cities. In such circumstances any situation which called for the removal of a large number of able-bodied men to fight abroad can only have created further havoc.

How Britain in general, and the Regni in particular, fared against this darkening economic backcloth is difficult to say, except that they are unlikely to have escaped its major effects. The defensive measures taken by the inhabitants of Chichester may be seen, in part at least, as a reflection of the need for the greater protection of the urban community against a troubled countryside. Similarly it could be argued that the change in the life-style of the two Chilgrove villas late in the fourth century implies the migration of their owners into the safety of the city, leaving their estates to be worked by bailiffs. Such speculations, while plausible, are impossible to prove.

In the countryside it is possible to see something of the breakdown of peasant life. While large numbers of farmsteads existed in the first and second centuries, very few indeed survived into the second half of the fourth. Those that did tended to be the larger nucleated villages like the Chalton village, or the village at Thundersbarrow[9] (p. 101). Nucleation of this kind must be the result of socio-economic pressures. Some of the villages may indeed have been deliberately created for the farm labourers (*coloni*) belonging to the large estates, and sited in the heart of the farmland rather than close to the villa itself. Such an arrangement would have been both efficient, in cutting down travelling time, and expedient, in keeping a potentially dangerous labour-force split up and at a distance.

Even if nucleation of peasant population explains in part the relative dearth of late-fourth-century settlement, the general fact of massive population decline must have had a dramatic and lasting effect on the countryside. By the late fourth century large tracts of Downland were reverting once more to waste.

The formal end of Roman Britain came about in 410 in a complex of interwoven events unlikely ever to fully be understood. With the last remnants of the army gone three years before, Britain was defenceless. In 410 the Saxons mounted an attack of some severity. The historian Zosimus records (IV 5) what followed: 'The Britons took up arms, and braving danger for their own independence, freed their cities from the barbarians threatening them: and all Armorica and the other provinces of Gaul copied the British example and freed themselves in the same way, expelling their Roman governors and establishing a state of their own as best they could.'

In the same year the towns of Britain received a letter from the Emperor Honorius, no doubt in reply to a plea from them, telling them to 'look after their own defence'. Taken on the simplest level, these sources imply the total overthrow of the central administration followed by a reversion to local rule by the cities. Such a view is consistent with the words of Procopius when he says that Britain from now on was ruled by tyrants. What part the peasants played in this crucial year is unclear. It has been argued that the overthrow of the government was the result of a massive peasant uprising aimed at destroying not only the law but the cities as well, and it was to this that Honorius' letter referred.[10] While such a view has much to commend it, it is difficult to prove: all that can safely be said is that social revolution, if never a reality, must always have been a potential danger.

For about twenty years it seems that an uneasy peace was maintained by the local leaders who emerged from the ranks of the urban aristocracy, but towards the end of this time the Picts and Scots again became troublesome. Some time about 430 Vortigern, who is described by the writer Gildas as *superbus tyrannus*, implying some kind of general overlordship, decided to adopt the well-tried Roman practice of employing Germanic mercenaries to protect the British shores.[11] This, according to Gildas, followed the outbreak of a great plague which had presumably depleted the available man-power to a frighteningly low level. Seen in this light, and against the background of established Roman policy, Vortigern's act of bringing in mercenaries was unexceptional: indeed it may have been the only course of action open to him.

The policy worked adequately for a while so long as the mercenaries were well paid; but in 442, claiming that they were being under provided, they rebelled and moved out of their treaty territories to overrun the country. They did not stop, says Gildas, 'until, destroying the neighbouring towns and lands (they) reached the other side of the island, and dipped (their) red and savage tongue in the Western Ocean'. It was in about 446, in this period of devastation and turmoil that the famous message known as 'the Groans of the Britons' was sent to the Roman general Aetius, who at the time was campaigning in Gaul: 'The barbarians drive us to the sea, the sea drives us to the barbarians. Between the two means of death we are either killed or drowned.' Aetius did not respond.[12]

The story so far has been pieced together using the few

scraps of available documentary evidence. Against this framework the archaeological evidence must now be examined. At Portchester the picture of the early-fifth-century occupation is clear.[13] Alongside the Roman streets three *grubenhauser* (huts with sunken floors) have been found, belonging to a well defined Germanic style quite alien to the tradition of Roman building (fig. 44). In one *grubenhaus* was found a quantity of pottery of a type recorded on the continent in early-fifth-century contexts, together with a gilded bronze disc brooch decorated in repoussée, the closest parallels for which lie in Frankish material of the late fourth and early fifth centuries. In addition to the *grubenhauser* the settlement also included several post-built huts and a well in which was discovered an early-fifth-century purse mount. The evidence is therefore strongly suggestive of the presence of a Germanic mercenary detachment in Portchester in the early part of the fifth century. It is tempting to see it as one of the bands settled by Vortigern in the 430s to guard the coast, much as the Roman troops had done up to 60 years before.

Chichester, on the other hand, has practically nothing to tell us about its fortunes during the fifth century. A coin of Valentinian III (425-55), however, hints at continued occupation and it may reasonably be supposed that the town served as a centre for local government, perhaps ruled by its own tyrant, at least until the Saxon revolt of 442. Thereafter its history is obscure. Although it is dangerous to argue from the absence of evidence, the fact that no fifth-century Germanic material has been found in the town in spite of extensive excavations, taken together with the observation that the land for at least ten miles around is without trace of fifth-century cemeteries or occupation, could suggest that the sub-Roman population continued to maintain their own order without the need to employ mercenaries.

If, then, Portchester was defended by mercenaries in the early fifth century, while Chichester continued to look after its own defence, the question of the organization of the remainder of the Sussex coastal plain is immediately raised.[14] Did Pevensey, for example, follow Portchester or Chichester? We have little direct evidence, but the dense

Fig. 44. A Saxon *grubenhaus* inside the shore fort at Portchester

occupation of the fort in the last decades of the Roman era and the absence of fifth-century Germanic finds would tend to suggest that as a centre of nucleated settlement it continued to be maintained by its native population. It may be that the fort protected a substantial adjacent territory, perhaps as far west as the River Cuckmere, an area so far providing no trace of early Germanic settlement.

The area between the Arun and the Cuckmere was without a late-Roman walled settlement to serve as a natural focus for defensive activities, but it does yield considerable evidence of Germanic activity which may reasonably be dated to the early part of the fifth century. At Highdown, a site which we have seen was re-defended late in the Roman period and quite probably garrisoned, an extensive cemetery began to develop, eventually containing both inhumation and cremation burials. Among the very rich grave goods were found a number of pieces of elaborately decorated metalwork, all decorated in what has been called the Quoit Brooch style.[15] A detailed study of this metalwork strongly suggests that it was made for an aristocratic section of the population, possibly a military hierarchy, with evident Germanic taste, and that it should be dated to the period 400-50. In addition to the early metal objects, the Highdown cemetery has yielded two other classes of early-fifth-century artifacts: pottery and glass. The earliest pots were of biconical type,[16] sometimes with rillings above the shoulder or with the shoulder moulded into a series of facets, in the style of vessels found in quantity in the Low Countries in contexts dating before the middle of the century. While these types could have continued to be used in Britain after 450, their presence at Highdown can be taken to support an early-fifth-century origin for the cemetery. The glass is even more impressive.[17] Five of the vessels recovered are considered to be of late-Roman origin and, since the very nature of the material would make them most unlikely to survive long after the end of the Roman period, it is reasonable to suggest burial in the decades before 450. The rest of the glass is of Saxon type, but none of it need date to after 500.

Taking the evidence of the metalwork, the pottery and the glass together, we may reasonably conclude that the Highdown cemetery represents, in its initial stages, the burial ground of a community of Germanic mercenaries who were settled in the area between 410 and 450. That Highdown had been re-fortified in the fourth century adds some weight to the view that the mercenaries were brought in by Vortigern as part of his general defence strategy, possibly in the 420s or 430s, to maintain the earlier policy of defending the block of Downs between the Arun and the Adur.

Turning now to the Downland between the Ouse and the Cuckmere, where there was some evidence to suggest earlier re-fortification of the Caburn, the presence of fifth-century mercenaries is even more dramatically demonstrated. No less than five cemeteries of fifth-century date are now known at Malling Hill, Beddington Hill, Bishopstone, Alfriston and Selmeston. Of these, Alfriston provides a direct parallel to Highdown with the same combination of early pottery, Quoit

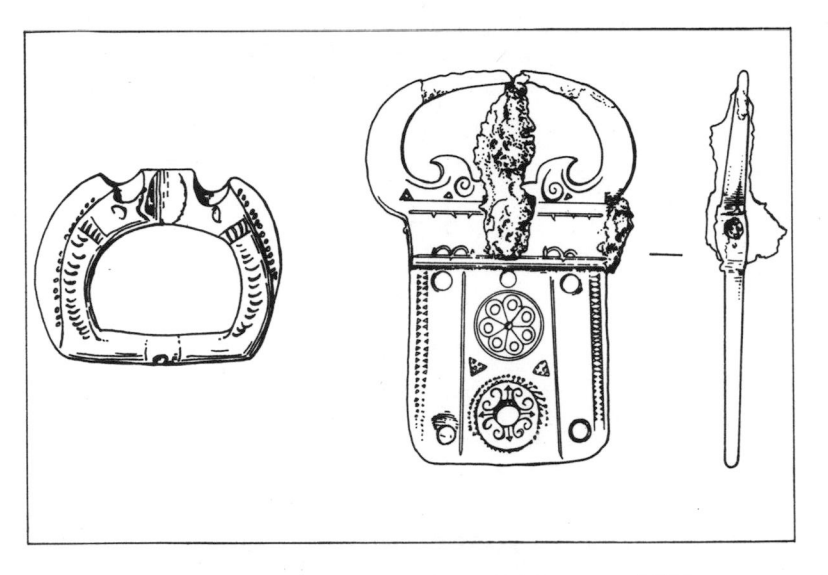

Fig. 45. Late-fourth-century buckles from Chichester and Bishopstone

Brooch style metalwork and late-Roman glassware. If High-down originates in about 420-30, so too must Alfriston. Bishopstone has also produced a bronze buckle decorated in the Quoit Brooch style (fig. 45), which points to an equally early origin, but the other sites have offered little to suggest an indisputable pre-450 beginning.[18]

The only remaining area to be considered is the strip of Downland between the Adur and the Ouse. No late-Roman fortifications are known, nor are there any recorded fifth-century finds, but it remains a possibility that the nucleated settlement at Hassocks continued to control the defence of the area after 410 in the same manner as we have suggested that the sub-Roman population of Chichester commanded its region at this time. The appearance of the place-name Wickham, just to the north of the Roman road junction, may be an added indication of the survival of a significant community into the Saxon period, but the matter is debatable.

What emerges from this lengthy and admittedly sometimes speculative discussion is a remarkably suggestive pattern. There would appear to be six distinct territories (fig. 46).

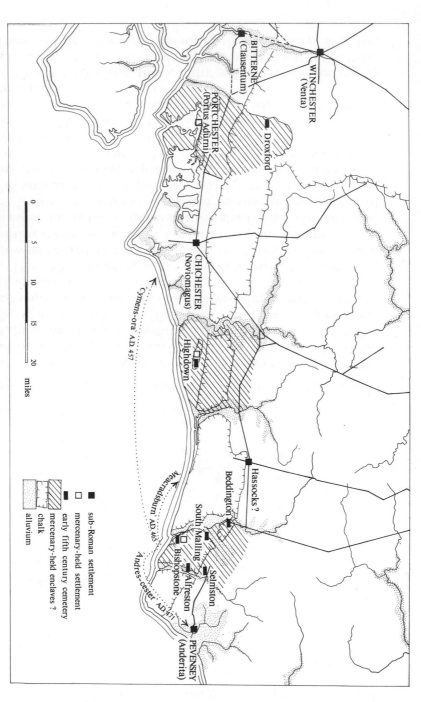

Fig. 46. Saxon and British enclaves in the territory of the Regni during the fifth century A.D.

Three of them — those centred on Chichester, Hassocks(?) and Pevensey — show no sign of early-fifth-century Germanic occupation; while those between, based on or near Portchester, Highdown and Alfriston/Bishopstone, all produce clear indications of well-established Germanic settlement. It is very tempting to see this as a reflection of the defensive policy of the sub-Roman leaders — the old nucleated settlements continuing to defend themselves while the intervening territories were put under the control of mercenary bands.

It is now generally accepted that this phase of controlled settlement lasted until 440-50, the period to which the Saxon rebellion so vividly described by Gildas belongs. This event seems also to be referred to by the *Gallic Chronicle* in an entry for the year 442, which states quite simply that 'Britain long troubled by various happenings and disasters passed under the authority of the Saxons'. The break-out of the Germanic mercenaries and the devastating effect it must have had on the last remnants of Romanized life was in all probability spread over a number of years. The *Anglo-Saxon Chronicle* lists three events impinging upon what was left of the Regni. In 477 Aella and his three sons, Cymen, Wlencing and Cissa, made a landing at a place known as Cymens-ora 'and slew there many Britons and drove some in flight into the wood called Andreds-lea'. Later, in 485, Aella fought the Britons on the bank of Mearcradsburn, and finally in 491 Aella and Cissa besieged Andreds-cester and slaughtered all the Britons who lived there.

The interpretation of so bald a narrative is difficult, not the least because of doubts as to the reliability of the dates. However, a recent detailed study of all the texts bearing upon Dark Age chronology has shown that these Sussex series, among others, are probably consistently 20 years too late.[19] Thus Cymens-ora becomes 457, Mearcradsburn 465, and Andreds-cester 471. Two of the three places at which Aella fought can be located with reasonable certainty: on the evidence of a later charter Cymens-ora is thought to be on the coast south of Chichester, while Andreds-cester must be Pevensey. Mearcradsburn is more difficult to place but probably means 'the river of the frontier agreed by treaty'.

It is surely significant that at least two of Aella's battles were fought in areas which on totally different grounds have been suggested to be sub-Roman enclaves, one based on Pevensey the other on Chichester. At both he was opposed by organized bands of Britons, and at both he appears to have imposed his domination. The third battle, on the river of the frontier agreed by treaty, could very easily refer to his attempt to overrun the third native-held territory, the river being either the Adur or the Ouse. The success of the campaign is unrecorded.

All the time that these military operations were being undertaken, the remnants of the sub-Roman population must have continued to extract a living from the soil. How large the population was cannot now be assessed, but with the natural decrease in birth-rate during the Roman period, the draining-off of the active man-power by the late Roman commanders and the great plague of the 420s or 430s, the countryside must have been drastically depleted of its population. This was, after all, the principal reason why Vortigern was forced to employ the mercenaries.

The recognition of sub-Roman settlement is very difficult, largely because of the lack of datable material. Coinage had gone out of regular use: very few copper coins reached Britain after 402; gold coins are virtually unknown after 406 and silver after 408. By 430 the coin-economy had completely broken down.[20] With the collapse of regular markets soon after 410 the great pottery manufacturing centres can hardly have maintained production. Thus, apart from outdated coins and a few surviving pots, the peasant communities and indeed the towns were without the use of closely datable artifacts.

If, however, one begins with the assumption that some kind of occupation must have continued in most of the areas that were densely settled at the end of the fourth century, the problem resolves itself into one of recognizing fifth-century occupation. One artifact which seems to be distinctive is a class of hand-made pottery tempered with chaff.[21] A range of simple forms have been found in the early fifth-century *grubenhaus* at Portchester, showing that manufacture had begun by about the 420s-430s, presumably to fill the gap left by the breakdown of the pottery monopolies. At

Chalton a few sherds of this grass-tempered ware have been discovered on the site of one of the fourth-century villages, hinting at the possibility of a continuation of village life well into the first half of the fifth century. Exactly the same sequence has been defined at Bishopstone where the late Roman village is overlaid by 'Saxon' occupation. Here, however, there may be a difference in that the fifth-century occupation appears to have a strong Germanic element. Bishopstone is more a parallel with Portchester than with Chalton.

The fate of the peasant community living in the Chalton village must remain unknown, but barely a quarter of a mile away on the same ridge-top there exists a very extensive 'Saxon' settlement with traces of industrial activity and well-built timber houses. That its occupants were the descendants of the sub-Roman population remains an attractive hypothesis. Their hill-top village was only a few yards away from a small farm occupied by the ancestors of the original Regni.

Piecing together the fragments of archaeological and documentary evidence for the century from 370 to 470 does seem to yield a remarkably consistent picture. First came the settlement of a number of Germanic mercenaries at Chichester and probably Pevensey, in order to strengthen the late Roman garrisons in, and soon after, 370. Then in the 420s-430s larger mercenary contingents were placed at Portchester, near Highdown and near Alfriston, and finally between 457-71 bands of mercenaries led by Aella overran the remaining areas. In exactly 100 years the Regni passed from a state of unity under Roman law through a phase of fragmentation not at all unlike the pre-Roman situation and back once more to apparent unified rule — but this time under the domination of a Saxon warlord.

Notes and references

1. TRIBAL TERRITORY AND THE PRE-ROMAN IRON AGE

1. For a general discussion of changing sea-level in south-eastern Britain, see Hawkes, S.C. 1968.
2. The archaeological development of Sussex is described in some detail in Curwen, E.C. 1954. Although the book is now many years out of date, it is still the basic work. Terminology and dating have changed considerably and several important new discoveries have been made, but Curwen's book still stands as a comprehensive descriptive account of the area.
3. Cunliffe, B. 1971 a.
4. Curwen, E.C. 1929 and 1931.
5. Piggott, S. 1930.
6. For a discussion of some of the implications, see Cunliffe, B. 1971.
7. Burstow, G.P. and Holleyman, G.A. 1957.
8. Cunliffe, B. 1970 a.
9. There is no adequate recent publication on the problems of Iron Age pottery but the matter is discussed in the author's forthcoming book *Iron Age Communities of Britain*.
10. Allen, D.F. 1961 summarizes the coin evidence for the whole period. His earlier work, Allen, D.F. 1944, is concerned largely with the dynasties as recognizable through the later coin issues.
11. Hawkes, C.F.C. 1968.
12. See footnote 9.
13. Stevens, C.E. 1951.
14. Boon, G.C. 1969.
15. Bradley, R. 1971.
16. Summarized in Allen, D.F 1961, 286-96.
17. For a more detailed discussion of this period in relation to Sussex, see Cunliffe, B. 1971 b, 10-17.

2. HISTORY: A.D. 43-367

1. A recent general account of the invasion and of subsequent
   Romano-British history is to be found in Frere, S.S. 1967.
2. Cunliffe, B. 1971 b, 13-14.
3. Tacitus, *Agricola* 14.
4. Suetonius, *Vesp.* 4.
5. The present state of knowledge, with reference to earlier discussion, is to be found in Rivet, A.L. F. 1970, 50, 78.
6. Suetonius, *Vesp.* 4.
7. Cunliffe, B. 1971 b, 35-46.
8. Cunliffe, B. 1971 b, 13-14.
9. Eutropius ix, 21.
10. Discoveries up to 1934 are discussed in Winbolt, S.E. 1935 a. See
    also Heron-Allen, E, 1933 (Selsey); Mattingly, H.B. 1967 (Goring-
    on-sea); Mattingly, H.B. and Lewis, G.D. 1964 (Worthing); Mat-
    tingly, H. 1939 (Hove).
11. For the life of Carausius, see White D.A. 1961, 19-32. Much of the
    rest of this work has been superseded.
12. Cunliffe, B. 1968.
13. Cunliffe, B. 1963; 1966 and 1969.
14. *RIB.* 220.
15. Cunliffe, B. 1968, 269-271.
16. , Peers, C. 1960; Bushe-Fox, J.P. 1932; Saltzman, L.F. 1907 and
    1908.
17. Winbolt, S.E. 1935 a.
18. *J. Roman Stud.* lix (1969), 230.

3. COMMUNICATIONS AND URBAN SETTLEMENT

1. A number of detailed papers have been published on the Roman
   roads of Sussex by Mr I.D. Margery in *Sussex Archaeol. Coll.* The
   principal results are summarized in his two books: Margary, I.D.
   1948, and 1955. For the recently discovered Chichester to
   Silchester road see Clarke, A. 1959.
2. *RIB.* 220.
3. Winbolt, S.E. 1935 b.
4. Cunliffe, B. 1971 b, 5-9.
5. The principal sources on Chichester include Winbolt, S.E. 1935 a,
   9-19, for a summary of the discoveries up to 1934; Hannah, I.C.
   1934; White, G.M. 1936 a and b; Cottrill, F. 1935; Clark, G.M.
   1939; Wilson, A.E. 1952, 1956, 1957 a, 1957 b, 1962; Holmes, J.
   1962 and 1965; Murray, K.M. E. and Cunliffe, B. 1962; Down, A.
   1966 and 1968; and Down, A. and Rule, M. 1971. Interim reports
   of more recent work have appeared in the duplicated reports of the
   Chichester Civic Society produced annually since 1966.
6. Rivet, A.L. F. 1970.

7. Down, A. and Rule, M. 1971, 48.
8. Unpublished in detail: information from the excavator Mr A. Down.
9. Down, A. and Rule, M. 1971, 53 ff.
10. Down, A. 1968 and duplicated interim reports; also information from the excavator.
11. *RIB*. 92.
12. Cottrill, F. 1935 and subsequently in the interim reports of the Chichester Civic Society; also Holmes, J. 1965, 8-10.
13. Down, A. and Rule, M. 1971, 16.
14. Down, A. and Rule, M. 1971, 137-8.
15. *RIB*. 91.
16. White, G.M. 1936 a.
17. Holmes, J. 1965; 10-13.
18. Holmes, J. 1965, 2-5, and later unpublished work.
19. For a general account of the walls and ramparts, see Wilson, A.E. 1957 b, but this is augmented and corrected in Holmes, J. 1962 and Down, A. and Rule, M. 1971, 143-52.
20. Down, A. and Rule, M. 1971, 143-7.
21. Wilson, A.E. 1962.
22. For a general summary, see Frere, S.S. 1967, 250-2.
23. Holmes, J. 1965, 5-7.
24. White, G.M. 1936 b; *RIB*: 89.
25. *RIB*. 90.
26. Reported largely in interim accounts published annually by the Chichester Civic Society. Excavations are still (1972) in progress.
27. Murray, K.M.E. and Cunliffe, B. 1962.
28. Down, A. and Rule, M. 1971, 127-41.
29. Holmes, J. 1965, 16 (mention only).
30. Clark, G.M. 1939.
31. Down, A. and Rule, M. 1971, 53-126.
32. *RIB*. 94, 95.
33. *RIB*. 93
34. All conveniently summarized in Winbolt, S.E. 1935 a.
35. Wilson, A.E. 1957 b; Holmes, J. 1962.
36. Hawkes, S.C. and Dunning, G.C. 1961.
37. Winbolt, S.E. 1927.
38. For summary see Winbolt, S.E. 1935 a, 63-4.
39. Winbolt, S.E. and Goodchild, R.G. 1937, 1940.
40. By Miss Jane Evans for the Worthing Museum: unpublished.
41. Summarized in Winbolt, S.E. 1935 a, 63-4.
42. Winbolt, S.E. 1935 a, 63.
43. Curwen, E.C. 1943.
44. Winbolt, S.E. 1923, 1924.
45. Information from Miss Elizabeth Lewis, Portsmouth City Museums.
46. Couchman, J.E. 1925.

4. RURAL SETTLEMENT

1. Cunliffe, B. 1971 b, 46-76.
2. Scott, L. 1938, 1939; Wilson, A.E. 1947.
3. Winbolt, S.E. 1932.
4. Praetorius, C.J. 1910.
5. Sutton, T. 1952.
6. Cunliffe, B. 1971 b, 77-153.
7. Norris, N.E.S. and Burstow, G.P. 1950.
8. Hanworth, R. 1968.
9. Duplicated interim reports by the excavator, Mr A. Down, have been published by the Chichester Civic Society annually since 1966.
10. Winbolt, S.E. and Herbert, G. 1925. For a brief summary of the recent excavations see *J. Roman Stud.* liii (1963), 155-6. The mosaic floors are described in Toynbee 1964.
11. Wolseley, G.R., Smith, R.A. and Hawley, W. 1927.
12. Note in *Britannia II* (1971), 284-5.
13. Work by the author: unpublished.
14. Bowen, H.C. and Fowler, P.J. 1966.
15. Curwen, E.C. 1933.
16. Burstow, G.P. and Wilson, A.E. 1936.
17. Holleyman, G.A. 1935 a.
18. Wilson, A.E. 1940, 1950.
19. Curwen, E.C. and Williamson, R.P.R 1931.
20. Holleyman, G.A. 1935 b.
21. Work in progress by the author: largely unpublished.
22. Wolseley, G.R., Smith, R.A. and Hawley, W. 1927.
23. Holleyman, G.A. 1936.
24. Hearne, E.J.F. 1936.
25. Burstow, G.P. and Wilson, A.E. 1936.
26. Parsons, W.J. and Curwen, E.C. 1933.
27. Winbolt, S.E. 1935 a.
28. Note in Winbolt, S.E. 1935 a, 51.
29. Mitchell, G.S. 1910.
30. Frere, S.S. 1940.

5. INDUSTRY AND THE ECONOMY

1. Holleyman, G.A. 1935 b.
2. Curwen, E.C. 1933.
3. Cunliffe, B. 1971 b (vol. 2), 376.
4. Manning, W.H. 1966.
5. Curwen, E.C. 935.
6. Norris, N.E.S. and Burstow, G.P. 1950.
7. Information from the excavator, Mr A. Down.
8. Winbolt, S.E. and Herbert, G. 1925.

9. Information from the excavator, Mr A. Down.
10. Winbolt, S.E. 1927, 105 ff.
11. Unpublished excavations by Mrs M. Rule.
12. I owe this point to Mr M. Fulford: publication pending.
13. Cunliffe, B. 1970 b, 67-8.
14. Curwen, E.C. 1933, 146-9.
15. Goodchild, R.G. 1937.
16. Figg, W. 1849.
17. Green, T.K. 1970.
18. Cunliffe, B. 1971 b (vol. 2), 41-9.
19. Scott, L. 1938.
20. Sutton, T. 1952.
21. Lowther, A.W.G. 1948.
22. For Purbeck marble and other stones from Fishbourne, see
    Cunliffe, B. 1971 b (vol. 2), 1-42.
23. For a general summary of iron-working sites in Sussex, see Winbolt,
    S.E. 1935 a, 29-32.
24. Cleere, H. 1970.
25. Brodribb, G. 1969.
26. Murray, K.M.E. and Cunliffe, B. 1962, 97.
27. Down, A. and Rule, M. 1971, 143.

6. THE LATE FOURTH AND FIFTH CENTURIES

1. For a general description of late Romano-British history, see Frere,
   S.S. 1967
2. Cunliffe, B. 1968, 265-7.
3. Cunliffe, B. 1963, 227; 1968, 64-5.
4. Cunliffe, B. 1968, 268-71.
5. Wilson, A.E. 1940, 1950.
6. Curwen, E.C. and Williamson, R.P.R. 1931.
7. Wilson, A.E. 1939, 203.
8. The re-defended hillforts of Sussex are discussed together in
   Wilson, A.E. 1942.
9. Curwen, E.C. 1933.
10. Thompson, E.A. 1956 (giving relevant texts in full).
11. Gildas, *Liber Querulus*.
12. Two important accounts of these events should be consulted:
    Hawkes, C.F.C. 1956 and Morris, J. 1965.
13. Cunliffe, B. 1969, 65-7, 1970 b, 67-70.
14. For a general discussion of these problems, see Welch, M.G. 1971.
    The present account differs from this in some points of detail but
    relies largely upon it.
15. Evison, V.I. 1965, 46-78; Evison, V.I. 1968.
16. Myres, J.N.L. 1969, 88 and 104.
17. Harden, D.B. 1956, 135.
18. Note in *Medieval Archeol.*, xii (1968), 161; Evison, V.I. 1968, 244.
19. Morris, J. 1965.

20. Sutherland, C.H.V. 1956. Cunliffe, B. 1970 b.
21. Cunliffe, B. 1970 b, 68.

Bibliography

Allen, D.F. (1944) The Belgic dynasties of Britain and their coins, *Archaeologia* 90, 1-46.

Allen, D.F. (1961) The origins of coinage in Britain: a reappraisal, in *Problems of the Iron Age in Southern Britain* ed. Frere, S.S. (London), 97-308.

Boon, G.C. (1969) Belgic and Roman Silchester: the excavations of 1954-8 with an excursus on the early history of Calleva, *Archaeologia* 102, 1-82.

Bowen, H.C. and Fowler, P.J. (1960) Romano-British rural settlements in Dorset and Wiltshire, in *Rural Settlement in Roman Britain* ed. Thomas, A.C. (London), 43-67.

Bradley, R. (1971) A field survey of the Chichester Entrenchments, in Cunliffe, B.W. *Excavations at Fishbourne* vol. 1 (London), 17-36.

Brodribb, G. (1969) Stamped tiles of the 'Classis Britannica', *Sussex Archaeol. Collect.* 102-25, 107.

Burstow, G.P. and Holleyman, G.A. (1957) Late Bronze Age settlement on Itford Hill, Sussex, *Proc. Prehist. Soc.* 23, 167-212.

Burstow, G.P. and Wilson, A.E. (1936) Excavation of a Celtic village on the Ladies' Golf Course, The Dyke, Brighton: 1935, *Sussex Archaeol. Collect.* 77, 193-201.

Bushe-Fox, J.P. (1932) Some notes on coast defences, *J. Roman Stud.* 22, 60-72.

Clark, G.M. (1939) The Roman cemetery at Chichester, *Sussex Archaoel. Collect.* 80, 171-92.

Clarke, A. (1959) The Chichester-Silchester Roman road, *Proc. Hampshire Fld. Club Archaeol Soc.* 22, 83-97.

Cleere, H. (1970) *The Romano-British Industrial Site at Bardown, Wadhurst.* (Chichester).

Cottrill, F. (1935) The new Post Office site (Chichester). *Sussex Archaeol. Collect.* 76, 159-71.

Couchman, J.E. (1925) A Roman cemetery at Hassocks, *Sussex Archaeol. Collect.* 66, 34-61.

Cunliffe, B. (1963) Excavations at Portchester Castle, Hants, 1961-3, *Antiq. J.* 43, 218-27.

Cunliffe, B. (1966) Excavations at Portchester Castle, Hants, 1963-5, *Antiq. J.* 46, 39-49.

Cunliffe, B. (1968) The British fleet, in *Fifth Report on the excavations of the Roman Fort at Richborough, Kent* ed. Cunliffe, B.W. (London), 55-71.

Cunliffe, B. (1969) Excavations at Portchester Castle, Hants, 1966-8, *Antiq. J.* 49, 62-74.

Cunliffe, B. (1970 a) A Bronze Age settlement at Chalton, Hants (site 78), *Antiq. J.* 50, 1-13.

Cunliffe, B. (1970 b) The Saxon culture-sequence at Portchester Castle, *Antiq. J.* 50, 67-85.

Cunliffe, B. (1971 a) Some aspects of hillforts and their cultural environments, in Hill, D. and Jesson, M. (eds.) *The Iron Age and its Hill-forts* (Southampton), 53-70.

Cunliffe, B. (1971 b) *Excavations at Fishbourne* (2 vols.) (London).

Curwen, E.C. (1929) Excavations in the Trundle Goodwood 1928, *Sussex Archaeol. Collect.* 70, 33-85.

Curwen, E.C. (1931) Excavations in the Trundle, *Sussex Archaeol. Collect.* 72, 100-50.

Curwen, E.C. (1933) Excavations on Thundersbarrow Hill, Sussex, *Antiq. J.* 13, 109-51.

Curwen, E.C. (1943) Roman lead cistern from Pulborough, Sussex, *Antiq. J.* 23, 155-7.

Curwen, E.C. (1954) *The Archaeology of Sussex* (London).

Curwen, E.C. and Williamson, R.P.R. (1931) The date of Cissbury Camp, *Antiq. J.* 11, 13-36.

Down, A. (1966) Excavations in Tower Street, Chichester, 1965, *Sussex Archaeol. Collect.* 104, 46-55.

Down, A. (1968) Excavations in Chapel Street, Chichester, 1967, *Sussex Archaeol. Collect.* 106, 113-32.

Down, A. and Rule, M. (1971) *Chichester Excavations* vol. 1 (Chichester).

Evison, V.I. (1965) *The Fifth Century Invasions South of the Thames* (London).

Evison, V.I. (1968) Quoit style buckles, *Antiq. J.* 48, 231-49.

Figg, W. (1849) On the remains of a Roman building discovered at Wiston in 1848, *Sussex Archaeol. Collect.* 2, 313-5.

Frere, S.S. (1940) A survey of archaeology near Lancing, *Sussex Archaeol. Collect.* 81, 141-72.

Frere, S.S. (1967) *Britannia* (London).

Goodchild, R.G. (1937) The Roman brickworks at Wykehurst Farm in the parish of Cranleigh, *Surrey Archaeol. Collect.* 45, 74-115.

Green, T.K. (1970) Roman tileworks at Itchingfield, *Sussex Archaeol. Collect.*, 108, 23-38.

Hannah, I.C. (1934) The walls of Chichester, *Sussex Archaeol. Collect.* 75, 107-29.

Hanworth, R. (1968) The Roman villa at Rampsley, Ewhurst, *Sussex Archaeol. Collect.* 65, 1-70.

Harden, D.B. (1956) Glass vessels in Britain and Ireland, A.D. 400-1000, in *Dark-Age Britain* ed. Harden, D.B. (London), 132-70.

Hawkes, C.F.C. (1956) The Jutes of Kent, in *Dark-Age Britain* ed. Harden, D.B. (London), 91-111.

Hawkes, C.F.C. (1968) New thoughts on the Belgae, *Antiquity* 42, 6-16.

Hawkes, S.C. (1968) The physical geography of Richborough, in *Fifth Report on the Excavations of the Roman Fort at Richborough, Kent* ed. Cunliffe, B.W. (London), 224-30.

Hawkes, S.C. and Dunning, G.C. (1961) Soldiers and settlers in Britain, fourth to fifth century, *Medieval Archaeol.* 5, 1-70.

Hearne, E.J.F. (1936) 'Shepherds Garden', Arundel Park, *Sussex Archaeol. Collect.* 77, 222-43.

Heron-Allen, E. (1933) A hoard of Roman coins from a villa-site at Selsey, *Sussex Archaeol. Collect* 74, 140-63.

Holleyman, G.A. (1935 a) Romano-British site on Wolstonbury Hill, *Sussex Archaeol Collect.* 76, 35-45.

Holleyman, G.A. (1935 b) The Celtic field-system in South Britain, *Antiquity* 9, 443-54.

Holleyman, G.A. (1936) An early British agricultural village site on Highdole Hill, near Telscombe, *Sussex Archaeol. Collect.* 77, 202-21.

Holmes, J. (1962) The defences of Roman Chichester, *Sussex Archaeol. Collect.* 80-92, 100.

Holmes, J. (1965) *Chichester: the Roman Town* (Chichester).

Lowther, A.W.G. (1948) *A Study of the Patterns on Roman Flue Tiles and their Distribution* (Farnham).

Manning, W.H. (1966) A group of bronze models from Sussex in the British Museum, *Antiq. J.* 46, 50-9.

Margary, I.D. (1948) *Roman Ways in the Weald* (London).

Margary, I.D. (1955) *Roman Roads in Britain* vol. 1 (London).

Mattingly, H. (1939) The Hove radiate hoard, *SNQ.*vii, 234-9.

Mattingly, H.B. (1967) A hoard of 'Barbarous radiates' from Goring-on-Sea, *Sussex Archaeol. Collect.* 105, 56-61.

Mattingly, H.B. and Lewis, G.D. (1964) A hoard of Barbarous radiates from Mill Road, Worthing. *Numis. Chron.* 4, 189-99.

Mitchell, G.S. (1910) Excavations at Chanctonbury Ring, 1909, *Sussex Archaeol. Collect.* 53, 1909, 131-7.

Morris, J. (1965) Dark Age dates, in Jarret, M.G. and Dobson, B. (eds.) *Britain and Rome* (Kendal), 145-85.

Murray, K.M.E. and Cunliffe, B.W. (1962) Excavations at a site in North Street, Chichester, 1958-9, *Sussex Archaeol. Collect.* 100, 93-110.

Myres, J.N.L. (1969) *Anglo-Saxon Pottery and the Settlement of England* (Oxford).

Norris, N.E.S. and Burstow, G.P. (1950) A Prehistoric and Romano-British site at West Blatchington, Hove, *Sussex Archaeol. Collect.*

89, 1-56.

Parsons, W.J. and Curwen, E.C. (1933) An agricultural settlement on Charleston Brow, near Firle Beacon, *Sussex Archaeol. Collect.* 74, 164-80.

Peers, C. (1960) *Pevensey Castle, Sussex* (London).

Piggott, S. (1930) Butser Hill, *Antiquity* 4, 187-200

Praetorius, C.J. (1910) (Paper on the Roman building near Pulborough, Sussex), *Proc. Soc. Antiq.* London, 23, 121-9.

Rivet, A.L.F. (1970) The British section of the Antonine Itinerary, *Britannia 1*, 34-82.

Saltzman, L.F. (1907) *Excavations on the site of the Roman fortress at Pevensey* (London).

Saltzman, L.F. (1908) *Excavations at Pevensey* (London).

Scott, L. (1938) The Roman villa at Angmering, *Sussex Archaeol. Collect.* 3-44, 79

Scott, L. (1939) Angmering Roman villa, 80, 89-92

Stevens, C.E. (1951) Britain between the invasions, in *Aspects of Archaeology in Britain and Beyond* ed. Grimes, W.F. (London), 332ff.

Sutherland, G.H.V. (1956) Coinage in Britain in the fifth and sixth centuries, in *Dark Age Britain* ed. Harden, D.B. (London), 3-10.

Sutton, T. (1952) The Eastbourne Roman villa, *Sussex Archaeol. Collect. 90, 1-12.*

Thompson, E.A. (1956) Zosimus on the end of Roman Britain, *Antiquity* 30, 163-7.

Toynbee, J.M.C. (1964) *Art in Britain under the Romans* (Oxford).

Welch, M.G. (1971) Late Romans and Saxons in Sussex, in *Britannia* II, 232-7.

White, D.A. (1961) *Litus Saxonicum* (Wisconsin).

White, G.M. (1936 a) The Chichester amphitheatre: preliminary excavations, *Antiq. J.* 16, 149-59.

White, G.M. (1936 b) A new Roman inscription from Chichester, *Antiq. J.* 16, 461-4.

Wilson, A.E. (1939) Excavations at the Caburn, 1938, *Sussex Archaeol. Collect.* 80, 193-213.

Wilson, A.E. (1940) Report on the excavations at Highdown Hill, Sussex, August 1939, *Sussex Archaeol. Collect.* 81, 173-204.

Wilson, A.E. (1942) The end of Roman Sussex and the early Saxon settlement, *Sussex Archaeol. Collect.* 82, 35-58.

Wilson, A.E. (1947) Angmering Roman villa, *Sussex Archaeol. Collect.* 86, 1-21.

Wilson, A.E. (1950) Excavations on Highdown Hill, 1947. *Sussex Archaeol. Collect.* 89, 163-78.

Wilson, A.E. (1952) Chichester excavations 1947-50, *Sussex Archaeol. Collect.* 90, 164-200.

Wilson, A.E. (1956) The beginnings of Roman Chichester, *Sussex Archaeol. Collect.* 94, 100-43.

Wilson, A.E. (1957 a) Roman Chichester, *Sussex Archaeol. Collect.* 95,

106-43.

Wilson, A.E. (1957 b) *The Archaeology of the Chichester City Walls* (Chichester).

Wilson, A.E. (1962) North Walls and Northgate, *Sussex Archaeol. Collect.* 100, 75-9.

Winbolt, S.E. (1923) Alfoldean Roman station, *Sussex Archaeol. Collect.* 64, 81-104.

Winbolt, S.E. (1924) Alfoldean Roman station: second report (on 1923), *Sussex Archaeol. Collect.* 65, 112-57.

Winbolt, S.E. (1927) Excavations at Hardham Camp, Pulborough, April 1926, *Sussex Archaeol. Collect.* 68, 89-132.

Winbolt, S.E. (1932) Roman villa at Southwick, *Sussex Archaeol. Collect.* 73, 13-32.

Winbolt, S.E. (1935 a) Romano-British Sussex, in *Victoria County History of Sussex* vol. 3 ed. Saltzman, L.F. (London).

Winbolt, S.E. (1935 b) Remains of the Roman bridge over the Arun, Alfoldean, *Sussex Archaeol. Collect.* 76, 183-92.

Winbolt, S.E. and Goodchild, R.G. (1937) A Roman villa at Lickfold, Wiggonholt, *Sussex Archaeol. Collect.* 78, 13-36.

Winbolt, S.E. and Goodchild, R.G. (1940) The Roman villa at Lickfold, Wiggonholt, *Sussex Archaeol. Collect.* 81, 55-67.

Winbolt, S.E. and Herbert, G. (1925) *The Roman Villa at Bignor, Sussex* (Chichester).

Wolseley, G.R., Smith, R.A., and Hawley, W. (1927) Prehistoric and Roman settlements on Park Brow, *Archaeologia*, 76, 1-40.

Index